GRADE 3

everyday

Vocabulary

Intervention Activities

MW00332792

Table of Contents

Using Everyday Vocabulary Intervention Activities

Current research identifies vocabulary and word study as essential skills for reading success. Before children learn to read, they need to be aware of the meaning of words. Vocabulary instruction teaches children how to determine the meanings of words by utilizing contextual and conceptual clues. Word-study and word-solving strategies help children build their vocabularies, which leads to increased reading comprehension.

Effective vocabulary activities provide students with opportunities to:

• Actively engage in learning more about words and how words work

• Build their vocabularies and gain greater control of language

• Develop the ability to use context clues to define unfamiliar words

• Develop and build content vocabulary

Although some students master these skills easily during regular classroom instruction, many others need additional re-teaching opportunities to master these essential skills. The Everyday Vocabulary Intervention Activities series provides easy-to-use, five-day intervention units for Grades K–5. These units are structured around a research-based Model-Guide-Practice-Apply approach. You can use these activities in a variety of intervention models, including Response to Intervention (RTI).

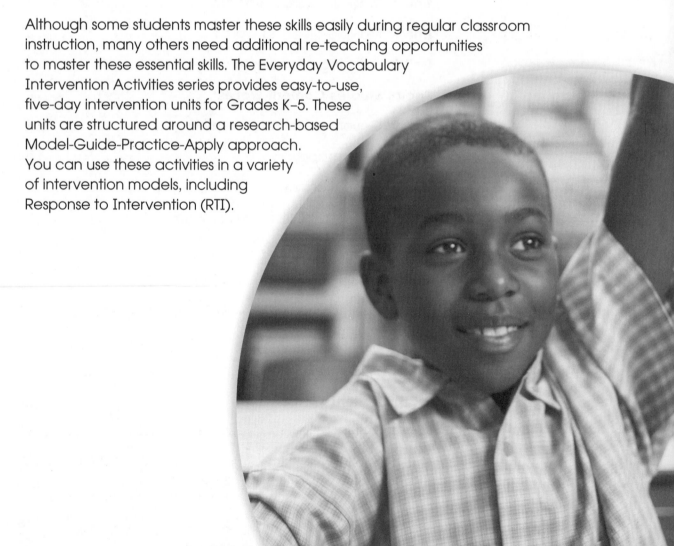

Getting Started

In just five simple steps, *Everyday Vocabulary Intervention Activities* provides everything you need to identify students' needs and to provide targeted intervention.

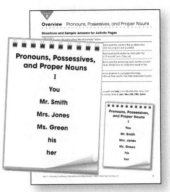

1. **PRE-ASSESS to identify students'** vocabulary needs.
Use the pre-assessment to identify the skills your students need to master.

2. **MODEL the skill.**
Every five-day unit targets a specific vocabulary and word study. On Day 1, use the teacher prompts and reproducible activity page to introduce and model the skill.

Day 1

Day 2

Day 3

Day 4

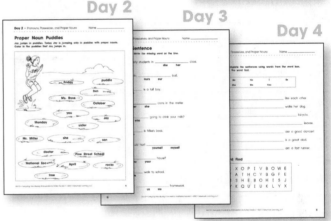

3. **GUIDE, PRACTICE, and APPLY.**
Use the reproducible practice activities for Days 2, 3, and 4 to build students' understanding and skill-proficiency.

Day 5

4. **MONITOR progress.**
Administer the Day 5 reproducible assessment to monitor each student's progress and to make instructional decisions.

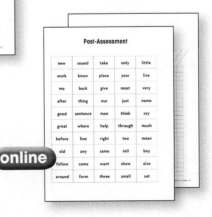

5. **POST-ASSESS to document student progress.**
Use the post-assessment to measure students' progress as a result of your interventions.

Standards-Based Vocabulary Awareness Skills in Everyday Intervention Activities

The vocabulary words and strategies found in the Everyday Intervention Activities series are introduced developmentally and spiral from one grade to the next. The chart below shows the types of words and skill areas addressed at each grade level in this series.

Everyday Vocabulary Intervention Activities Series Skills	K	1	2	3	4	5
Sight Words	✔	✔	✔	✔		
Nouns, Pronouns, and Proper Nouns	✔	✔	✔	✔	✔	✔
Verbs	✔	✔	✔	✔	✔	✔
Adjectives	✔	✔	✔	✔	✔	✔
Synonyms and Antonyms	✔	✔	✔	✔	✔	✔
Compound Words		✔	✔	✔	✔	✔
Multiple-Meaning Words	✔	✔	✔	✔	✔	✔
Classify Words by Subject	✔	✔	✔	✔	✔	✔
Word Analogies	✔	✔	✔	✔	✔	✔
Word Parts and Root Words	✔	✔	✔	✔	✔	✔
Word Webs and Diagrams	✔	✔	✔	✔	✔	✔
Using Words in Context	✔	✔	✔	✔	✔	✔
Using Context Clues to Determine Word Meaning				✔	✔	✔
Language Arts Content Words	✔	✔	✔	✔	✔	✔
Social Studies Content Words	✔	✔	✔	✔	✔	✔
Science Content Words	✔	✔	✔	✔	✔	✔
Math Content Words	✔	✔	✔	✔	✔	✔

Using Everyday Intervention for RTI

According to the National Center on Response to Intervention, RTI "integrates assessment and intervention within a multi-level prevention system to maximize student achievement and to reduce behavior problems." This model of instruction and assessment allows schools to identify at-risk students, monitor their progress, provide research-proven interventions, and "adjust the intensity and nature of those interventions depending on a student's responsiveness."

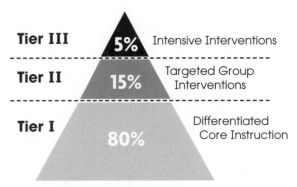

RTI models vary from district to district, but the most prevalent model is a three-tiered approach to instruction and assessment.

The Three Tiers of RTI	Using Everyday Intervention Activities
Tier I: Differentiated Core Instruction • Designed for all students • Preventive, proactive, standards-aligned instruction • Whole- and small-group differentiated instruction • Ninety-minute, daily core reading instruction in the five essential skill areas: phonics, phonemic awareness, comprehension, vocabulary, fluency	• Use whole-group vocabulary mini-lessons to introduce and guide practice with vocabulary strategies that all students need to learn. • Use any or all of the units in the order that supports your core instructional program.
Tier II: Targeted Group Interventions • For at-risk students • Provide thirty minutes of daily instruction beyond the ninety-minute Tier I core reading instruction • Instruction is conducted in small groups of three to five students with similar needs	• Select units based on your students' areas of need (the pre-assessment can help you identify these). • Use the units as week-long, small-group mini-lessons.
Tier III: Intensive Interventions • For high-risk students experiencing considerable difficulty in reading • Provide up to sixty minutes of additional intensive intervention each day in addition to the ninety-minute Tier I core reading instruction • More intense and explicit instruction • Instruction conducted individually or with smaller groups of one to three students with similar needs	• Select units based on your students' areas of need. • Use the units as one component of an intensive vocabulary intervention program.

Overview   Common Nouns

Directions and Sample Answers for Activity Pages

Day 1	See "Provide a Real-World Example" below.
Day 2	Read aloud the title and directions. Divide the class into small groups. Instruct groups to cut out one set of words, fold them, and put them in a container. Guide students to take turns picking a word. Remind them to state if they are a person, place, or thing, and then act out who or what they are.
Day 3	Read aloud the title and directions. Guide students to cut out and sort the words for places people go to have fun, travel, learn, or swim. Then show students how to glue words in the space for each category.
Day 4	Read aloud the title and directions. Help students read the clues and find the answer in the word box. Model how to write the word into the crossword puzzle.
Day 5	Read the directions aloud. Allow time for students to complete the tasks. Afterward, meet individually with students to discuss their results. Use their responses to plan further instruction and review.

Provide a Real-World Example

◆ Write **teacher** on chart paper. **Say:** *I am a teacher. A teacher is a person. The words naming people are nouns,* so the word *teacher is a noun.* Write **students** on chart paper. **Say:** *You are students. Students are people. So the word* **students** *is a noun, too.*

◆ Write **school**, **library**, **beach**, and **zoo** on the chart paper. **Ask:** *How are these words alike?* (Allow responses.) *They are all places. The names of places are nouns. What other places do you know?* Write students' responses on the chart paper.

◆ Point to the computer. **Say:** *A computer is a thing we use to get information. We also use a dictionary to get information.* Write **computer** and **dictionary** on the chart paper as you explain that the words for things are nouns, too. Invite students to look outside and **ask:** *What things do you see outside?* (Allow responses.) *Flowers, a rock, and grass are outdoor things.* Write **flowers**, **rock**, and **grass** on the chart paper. **Say:** *This week we will explore all types of nouns— people, places, and things.*

◆ Hand out the Day 1 activity page. **Say:** *Look at the first picture. The person is a firefighter. Find the word* **firefighter** *in the word list.* **Ask:** *Is a firefighter a person, a place, or a thing?* (Allow responses.) Then confirm that a firefighter is a person and check "person." Now direct attention to the second picture. **Say:** *This is the sun. Find the word* **sun** *in the word box.* Ask students if the sun is a person, place, or thing. Then check "thing." Repeat with the remaining pictures.

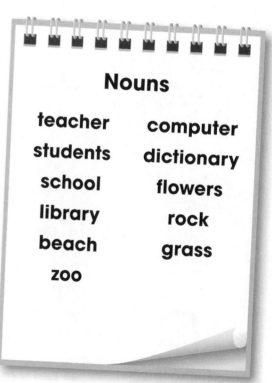

Nouns

teacher	computer
students	dictionary
school	flowers
library	rock
beach	grass
zoo	

Person, Place, or Thing?

**Look at each picture. Find the word in the word box. Then check "person,"
"place," or "thing."**

firefighter	bakery	doctor	sun	beach

❑ person   ❑ place   ❑ thing

❑ person   ❑ place   ❑ thing

❑ person   ❑ place   ❑ thing

❑ person   ❑ place   ❑ thing

❑ person   ❑ place   ❑ thing

Noun Charades

Cut out the words and fold them. Take turns picking a noun. State if you are a person, place, or thing. Then act out the noun. The player that guesses goes next.

baker	computer	cow	dictionary	firefighter
moon	newspaper	planet	playground	police officer
robot	sheep	train station	tree	zoo

Places, Places

Cut out the words. Sort them by places you go to have fun, travel, learn, or swim. Glue each one in the correct space.

Fun	**Travel**
Learn	**Swim**

airport	beach	bus station	lake	library
movie theater	playground	school	train station	zoo

Crossword

Read the clues. Find the answers in the word box. Write the answers in the crossword puzzle.

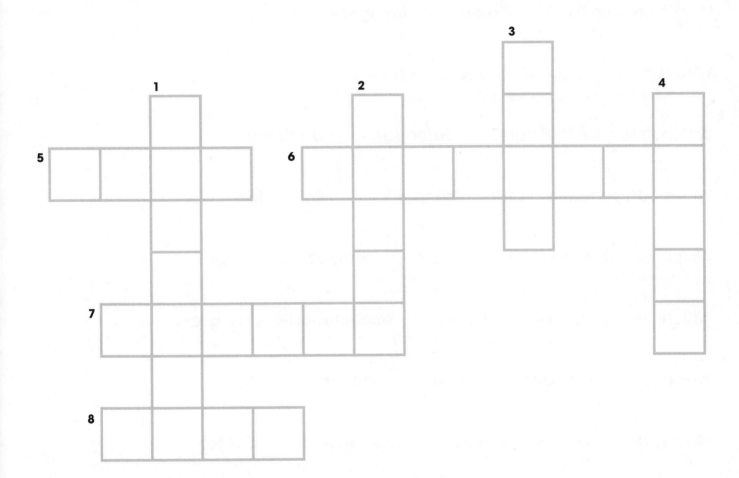

airport
baker
calendar
grass
mother
pond
soil
star

Clues

Down

1. Airplanes take off from here
2. A person who makes bread
3. You can swim in it
4. It grows out of the ground

Across

5. Another word for dirt
6. It tells you the month
7. Another name for mom
8. It twinkles in the nighttime sky

Assessment

Read each question. Draw a circle around the answer.

Who puts out fires?   **baker**   **firefighter**

Where can you swim?   **zoo**   **lake**

Which tells you the date?   **calendar**   **dictionary**

Where do teachers work?   **school**   **train station**

Which would you find in a library?   **computer**   **soil**

Which would you see in a park?   **encyclopedia**   **grass**

Which lives on a farm?   **sheep**   **baker**

Who takes care of sick people?   **bus driver**   **doctor**

Draw a picture of your family and label each member.

Overview   Pronouns, Possessives, and Proper Nouns

Directions and Sample Answers for Activity Pages

Day 1	See "Provide a Real-World Example" below.
Day 2	Read aloud the title and directions. Help students read the words in the puddles and identify the proper nouns. Guide them to color in the proper noun puddles.
Day 3	Read aloud the title and directions. Help students read each sentence and write the missing word on the line. (her, our, He, her, you, It, yourself, your, They, us)
Day 4	Read aloud the title and directions. Help students read the sentences and use the correct words in the word box to complete the sentences. Model how to circle the words in the word find.
Day 5	Read the directions aloud. Allow time for students to complete the tasks. Afterward, meet individually with students to discuss their results. Use their responses to plan further instruction and review.

Provide a Real-World Example

◆ Invite a volunteer to the front of the class. First point to yourself and **say:** *I am Ms./Mr./Mrs. (your last name)*. Point to the student and **say:** *You are (student's name)*. Write **I**, **you**, **Mrs./Mr./Ms. (your name)**, and **(student's name)** on chart paper. Point to the names and **say:** *Ms./Mr./Mrs. (your name) and (student's name) are proper nouns—nouns that name specific people, places, and things.* Explain the prefixes **Mr.**, **Mrs.**, and **Ms.**, including their pronunciation and when you use each. Encourage students to share other proper nouns they know. Write them on the chart paper.

◆ Point to a boy in the class. **Say:** *His name is (student's name)*. Point to a girl and **say:** *Her hair is brown.* Write **his** and **her** on the chart paper. Explain that **his** and **her** are possessive pronouns, or pronouns that show ownership.

◆ Hand out the Day 1 activity page. Read aloud the first sentence. Point out the pronoun **I**. Ask which picture shows this pronoun. Draw a circle around the picture. Repeat with the remaining sentences.

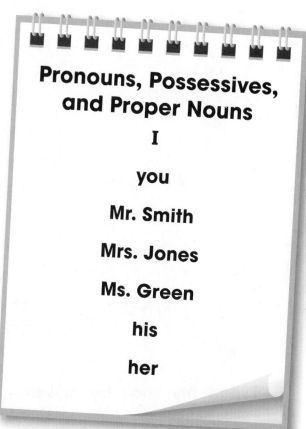

Pronouns, Possessives, and Proper Nouns

I

you

Mr. Smith

Mrs. Jones

Ms. Green

his

her

Circle the Picture

Draw a circle around the picture that shows the pronoun.

I fly a kite.   He reads a book.

She rides her bike.   They like to sing.

We dance.   Her dog is big.

I tied my shoe by myself.   They ate ice cream.

Proper Noun Puddles

Joy jumps in puddles. Today Joy is jumping in only puddles with proper nouns.
Color in the puddles that Joy jumps in.

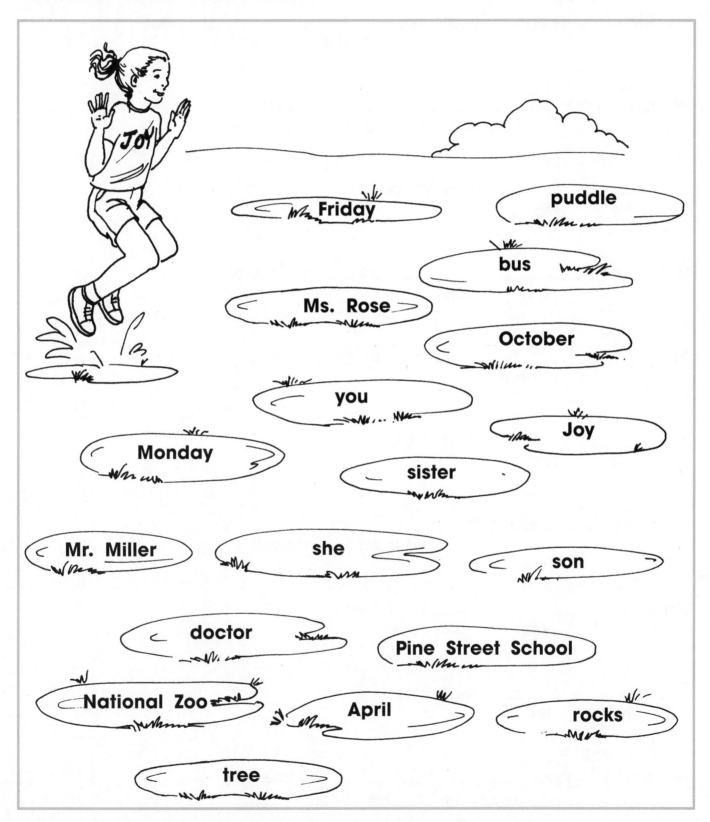

Finish the Sentence

Read the sentence. Write the missing word on the line.

Ms. Silver has twenty students in _____ class.

she   her

We play catch with _____ ball.

ours   our

_____ is a tall boy.

He   His

Molly put _____ coins in the meter.

her   she

Are _____ going to drink your milk?

I   you

_____ is Mike's book.

It   We

If you fall, you could hurt _____.

yourself   myself

Where is _____ house?

you   your

_____ walk to school.

They   Me

The teacher gave _____ homework.

us   we

Word Find

Read the clues. Complete the sentences using words from the word box. Circle the words in the word find.

He	his	I	its	She	We	You

Clues

_____ like each other.

_____ walks her dog.

He rides _____ bicycle.

The tree lost _____ leaves.

_____ are a good dancer!

_____ is a great dad.

_____ am a fast runner.

Word Find

I X O P I V B O W E

T A T H C Y B G F E

S S H E B O H I S J

Y K Q U I U K L Y X

Assessment

Draw a line from the picture to the correct pronoun.

he

they

she

it

Draw a line from the picture to the correct words.

our dog

its yarn

his hat

her book

Overview   Action Words

Directions and Sample Answers for Activity Pages

Day 1	See "Provide a Real-World Example" below.
Day 2	Read aloud the title and directions. Help students read each question and the answers. Guide them to draw a circle around the correct answer.
Day 3	Read aloud the title and directions. Help students read the sentence and write the verb that completes the sentence on the line.
Day 4	Read aloud the title and directions. Help students match the words in the two columns that mean the same thing.
Day 5	Read the directions aloud. Allow time for students to complete the task. Afterward, meet individually with students to discuss their results. Use their responses to plan further instruction and review.

Provide a Real-World Example

◆ Open a book and read aloud a few sentences. Then **say:** *I am reading. To* **read** *is a verb. A verb is a word that describes what a person or thing is doing, thinking, or feeling.* Write **read** on chart paper. **Ask:** *What do you do when I read aloud?* (Allow responses.) *You listen when I read.* **Listen** *is also a verb. It tells what you are doing.* Write **listen** on the chart paper. Ask students to share other verbs they know. Write their responses on the chart paper.

◆ **Say:** *When we read a story, sometimes we predict, or guess, what will happen next.* **Predict** *is a verb, too. Unlike reading and listening, you can't necessarily see someone predict, because it is happening in the person's head.* Write **predict** on the chart paper.

◆ Hand out the Day 1 activity page. **Say:** *Let's look at some verbs and decide if each one is a doing or thinking verb.* Draw students' attention to the word **fix. Say:** *When you fix something, like a bicycle or computer, you are doing something. Let's write the word* **fix** *in the "Doing" box.* Read aloud another verb: **understand. Say:** *You can't see someone understand something.* **Understand** *is a verb that describes what someone is thinking. Let's write* **understand** *in the "Thinking" box.* Repeat with the remaining verbs.

Action Words

read

listen

predict

Doing or Thinking?

Write verbs you can see someone doing in the "Doing" box. Write verbs that tell what someone is thinking in the "Thinking" box.

fix	understand	copy
decide	remember	research

Doing	**Thinking**

Circle the Answer

Read each question. Draw a circle around the word that answers the question.

Which do you listen to?	**music**	**map**
Which do you recite?	**poem**	**pond**
Where do you learn?	**shopping mall**	**school**
What do you operate?	**computer**	**cow**
Which do you read?	**brother**	**book**
Which do you avoid?	**daisy**	**danger**

Finish the Sentence

Read the sentence. Write the word that best completes it on the line.

Lucy _____ the flowers.
  arranged   **affected**

I do not _____ in the tooth fairy.
  conclude   **believe**

The actors _____ their lines.
  fix   **memorize**

If you want to do well in school, you need to _____.
  study   **insist**

If you don't study for the test, you will _____.
  fail   **succeed**

Nurses _____ doctors in caring for patients.
  operate   **assist**

Caterpillars _____ into butterflies.
  change   **model**

Max can't _____ what to eat for dessert.
  study   **decide**

Verb Match-Up

Draw a line to match verbs that have the same meaning.

ask	choose
assist	expect
decide	question
fix	recall
predict	repair
remember	support

Assessment

Complete each sentence. Draw a picture.

I read _____ .

I fix _____ .

I believe _____ .

I study _____ .

Overview Describing Words

Directions and Sample Answers for Activity Pages

Day 1	See "Provide a Real-World Example" below.
Day 2	Read aloud the title and directions. Help students match the words in the two columns that have opposite meanings.
Day 3	Read aloud the title and directions. Help students read the sentence and write the word that completes the sentence on the line.
Day 4	Read aloud the title and directions. Help students read the clues and find answers in the word box. Model how to write a word into the crossword puzzle.
Day 5	Read the directions aloud. Allow time for students to complete the task. Afterward, meet individually with students to discuss their results. Use their responses to plan further instruction and review.

Provide a Real-World Example

◆ Open the door very slowly and **say:** *I slowly open the heavy, dark door.* Write **slowly** on chart paper. **Ask:** *How did I open the door?* (Allow responses.) *I opened the door slowly. The word **slowly** describes an action—how I opened the door. Adverbs describe verbs, so **slowly** is an adverb.*

◆ **Ask:** *How did I describe the door?* (Allow responses.) *I described the door as heavy and dark.* Write **heavy** and **dark** on the chart paper. **Say:** *Heavy and dark are adjectives. Adjectives describe nouns. **Heavy** and **dark** describe the noun **door**.*

◆ Hand out the Day 1 activity page. Read aloud the directions and the first sentence. **Ask:** *Which word describes the mouse?* (Allow responses.) *Tiny describes the mouse. Remember, words that describe nouns are adjectives, so **tiny** is an adjective. Draw a circle around **tiny**.* Find and circle **tiny** in the Word Find. Read aloud the next sentence. **Ask:** *What does **quickly** describe?* (Allow responses.) *Quickly describes the verb **runs**. Remember, words that describe verbs are adverbs, so **quickly** is an adverb. Underline **quickly**.* Find and circle **quickly** in the Word Find. Repeat with the rest of the sentences.

**Describing Words:
Adjectives and Adverbs**

slowly

heavy

dark

Describing Word Identification

**Read each sentence. Find the describing word. Draw a circle around adjectives.
Underline adverbs. Then find the words in the Word Find below.**

I see a tiny mouse.

The girl runs quickly.

The enormous bear scared me.

He answered the question thoughtfully.

The baby sleeps peacefully.

Justin is the most valuable player on the team.

Word Find

```
T X O P L V B O W E N O R M O U S
I A T Q C V B G F E V V D S V V O
N S C Z B N Y K L J R O R X H A X
Y K Q U I C K L Y X O D T X I L K
T M P O N H V H M L P I U P O U L
E D T H O U G H T F U L L Y X A E
Y O P E R F H Y C B J P M E R B X
D E S A Q D O P E A C E F U L L Y
F L K J G B M K K L P U E R P E A
```

Opposites Attract

Draw a line to match describing words with opposite meanings.

quickly	cruelly
terrible	incomplete
loosely	light
valuable	shallow
nicely	slowly
deep	terrific
complete	tightly
dark	valueless

Finish the Sentence

Read the sentence. Write the adjective or adverb that best completes it on the line.

The president's speech was _____.

brief   **briefly**

The bird chirped _____.

cheerful   **cheerfully**

It was a _____ letter.

thoughtful   **thoughtfully**

Cross the street _____.

careful   **carefully**

The _____ princess lives in a castle.

beautiful   **beautifully**

Walk _____ or else you'll be late.

quick   **quickly**

The _____ monster showed his teeth.

terrible   **terribly**

The music played _____ in the background.

soft   **softly**

Crossword Puzzle

Read the clues. Find the answers in the word box. Write the answers in the crossword puzzle.

ancient

brief

colorful

hopeless

joyful

lively

shallow

valueless

Clues

Down

1. with lots of color
2. very happy
3. very old
4. not deep
5. lasting a short time

Across

6. without hope
7. to have no value or worth
8. full of life

Assessment

Draw a picture in each section to show the meaning of the describing word.

Draw something heavy.	Draw something you do carefully.
Draw something peaceful.	Draw something you do softly.

Overview   Contractions and Compounds

Directions and Sample Answers for Activity Pages

Day 1	See "Provide a Real-World Example" below.
Day 2	Read aloud the title and directions. Divide the class into pairs. Help students cut out the words and lay them facedown in rows. Model how to play the game.
Day 3	Read aloud the title and directions. Cut out one set of words for the class. Fold the words and put them into a container. Have each student pick a word. Guide them to walk around the room to find the other half of their compound word. Encourage pairs to come up with a sentence using their word.
Day 4	Read aloud the title and directions. Help students match the words in the two columns to make a compound word.
Day 5	Read the directions aloud. Allow time for students to complete the tasks. Afterward, meet individually with students to discuss their results. Use their responses to plan further instruction and review.

Provide a Real-World Example

◆ **Say:** *I'm writing on the chalkboard* as you write that sentence on the chalkboard. Point to the word **I'm** and **say: I'm** *is a contraction—two words combined with an apostrophe. What are the two words in* **I'm**? (Allow responses.) **I'm** *is a combination of the words* **I** *and* **am** *with an apostrophe.* Write **I** and **am** on the board, underneath the word **I'm** in the sentence. Then show students how to make the contraction by replacing the **a** in **am** with an apostrophe and pushing the words together to create **I'm**. Write **I'm** on chart paper.

◆ Now point to the word **chalkboard** in the sentence you wrote. **Say:** *Chalkboard* *is made up of two words, too. What two words are in* **chalkboard**? (Allow responses.) *Chalkboard* *is made of the words* **chalk** *and* **board**. *Chalkboard* *is an example of a compound word. Compound words are the combination of two separate words.* Write **chalkboard** on the chart paper. Point to the chart paper. Add the word **chart paper** to the list. Point out that **chart paper** is also a compound word, but that there is space between the two words. **Say:** *Chart paper* *is an open compound word.* *Chalkboard* *has no space between the words. It is a closed compound word.*

Compounds and Contractions

I'm

chalkboard

chart paper

◆ Hand out the Day 1 activity page. Read aloud the title and directions. Then read the first sentence. **Say:** *Snowball* *is a compound word. Let's write it on the line. The two words that make* **snowball** *are* **snow** *and* **ball**. *I will write these words on either side of the plus sign.* Read the next sentence. **Say:** *He's* *is a contraction. Let's write it on the line.* **He's** *is made of the words* **he** *and* **is**. *Let's write those in the equation.* Repeat these steps with the remaining sentences.

Word Add-Traction

Find the compound word or contraction in each sentence. Write the word on the line and the two smaller words that form it.

Joe threw a snowball.

_____ = _____ + _____

He's my brother.

_____ = _____ + _____

We go outside during a fire drill.

_____ = _____ + _____

I haven't seen that movie yet.

_____ = _____ + _____

Our playground has ten swings!

_____ = _____ + _____

I'm the tallest kid in class.

_____ = _____ + _____

You'll never believe what happened!

_____ = _____ + _____

Are you scared of thunderstorms?

_____ = _____ + _____

We flew in an airplane.

_____ = _____ + _____

It's hard to see in the dark.

_____ = _____ + _____

Contraction Concentration

Cut out the words and lay them facedown in rows. Try to match a contraction with its two words. If you make a match, keep the cards and take another turn. If no match, it's the next player's turn.

cannot	can't	do not	don't	does not
doesn't	I have	I've	is not	isn't
we will	we'll	she is	she's	should not
shouldn't	who is	who's	you're	you are

Compound Word Connection

Draw a word from the container. Walk around the room and find a word that, along with your word, makes a compound word. Together, come up with a sentence using the compound word.

air	cake	cup	boat	box
break	brush	cycle	door	fast
knob	lap	lunch	melon	motor
plane	sail	top	tooth	water

Match-Up

Draw a line to match up the words in the columns that make compound words.

book	be
every	book
mean	cycle
out	one
some	mate
note	rise
may	shelf
motor	side
room	where
sun	while

Assessment

Read the sentence. Write the word that best completes it on the line.

_____ your teacher.

     I'm   **I'd**

_____ go out later today.

     We'll   **We've**

_____ your teacher?

     Who'd   **Who's**

I _____ believe you!

     don't   **doesn't**

Look at the pictures. Write the compound word on the line.

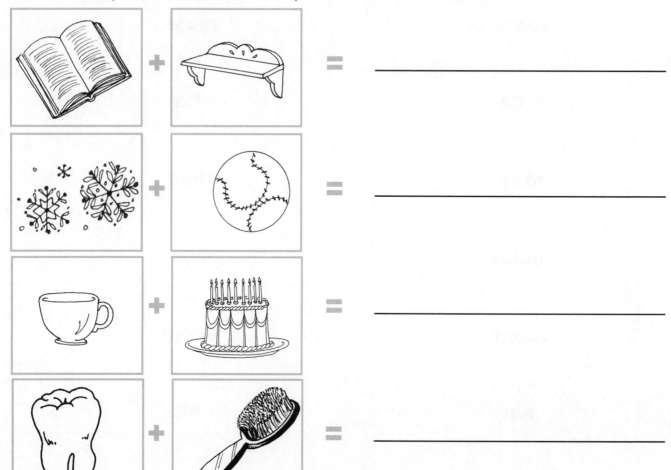

Overview   Synonyms and Antonyms

Directions and Sample Answers for Activity Pages

Day 1	See "Provide a Real-World Example" below.
Day 2	Read aloud the title and directions. Help students read the sentences. Remind them that synonyms are words that have the same or almost the same meaning. Guide them to find a synonym for each underlined word.
Day 3	Read aloud the title and directions. Remind students that antonyms are words with opposite meanings. Help them find the two words in each sentence that are antonyms, and draw a circle around them.
Day 4	Read aloud the title and directions. Divide the class into pairs. Help them choose a game board. Remind them that when writing X or O, they are also to write a synonym or antonym. Have pairs share their antonyms and synonyms with the rest of the class after they play.
Day 5	Read the directions aloud. Allow time for students to complete the task. Afterward, meet individually with students to discuss their results. Use their responses to plan further instruction and review.

Provide a Real-World Example

Synonyms for Happy
cheerful
blissful
joyful
Antonyms for Happy
sad
unhappy
cheerless
joyless

◆ Stand in front of the class with a big smile and **say:** *I feel happy today!* Write **happy** on chart paper. Ask students what other words mean the same thing as **happy**. Write students' responses on the chart paper under the heading "Synonyms." **Say:** *Words with almost the same meaning are called synonyms. Some synonyms for **happy** are **cheerful**, **blissful**, and **joyful**.* Write **cheerful**, **blissful**, and **joyful** on the chart paper.

◆ Now **say:** *Today I am happy, but yesterday I was sad.* Write **sad** on the chart paper. **Say:** *Words that have opposite meanings, such as **happy** and **sad**, are called antonyms. What are some other antonyms for **happy**?* Write students' responses under "Antonyms" on the chart paper. **Say:** *Some antonyms for **happy** are **unhappy**, **cheerless**, and **joyless**.* Write **unhappy**, **cheerless**, and **joyless** on the chart paper. Point to **unhappy** and **say:** *Adding the prefix **un-** to **happy** changed its meaning to the opposite.* Point to **cheerless** and **joyless** on the chart paper. **Say:** *Changing the suffix **-ful** to **-less** changed the meaning of these words to their opposite meanings.*

◆ Hand out the Day 1 activity page. Read aloud the title and directions. Then read the first word pair. **Say:** *Hopeful means "full of hope." **Hopeless**, however, means "without hope." These words are opposites, so I will check "Antonym." The suffixes **-ful** and **-less** are clues that the words are antonyms.* Now read the second word pair. **Say:** *The prefix **un-** is a clue. It means "not," so **unbelievable** means "not believable." This is the opposite of **believable**, so I will check "Antonym."* Now read the third pair. **Say:** *Huge and enormous both mean "big." I will check "Synonym."* Repeat with the remaining words.

Check It!

Read each word pair. Check the "Antonym" or "Synonym" box.

	Antonym	Synonym
hopeful/hopeless	❑	❑
unbelievable/believable	❑	❑
huge/enormous	❑	❑
brief/short	❑	❑
thoughtful/thoughtless	❑	❑
ancient/old	❑	❑
beautiful/ugly	❑	❑
warm/cool	❑	❑
full/empty	❑	❑
middle/center	❑	❑

Synonym Search

**Read each sentence. Find a synonym for the underlined word in the word box.
Write it on the line.**

damp	enormous	frightening	hot	incorrect
mean	nearly	noisy	priceless	young

The diamond ring is <u>valuable</u>. _____

It is <u>almost</u> time for bed. _____

The summer sun is <u>warm</u>. _____

The <u>youthful</u> woman is riding a bicycle. _____

The fireworks are <u>loud</u>. _____

That is the <u>wrong</u> answer. _____

The horror movie was <u>scary</u>. _____

Maya's hair is <u>wet</u>. _____

The <u>unfriendly</u> cat hissed at me. _____

The <u>huge</u> dog does not fit in his doghouse. _____

Antonyms, Antonyms Everywhere

Read each sentence and find the antonyms. Draw a circle around them.

A tiny mouse chased an enormous elephant.

The race starts at the school and ends at the park.

The dog happily ate the cookie as the girl looked on angrily.

Summer days are long, while winter days are brief.

The winner was joyful and the loser was joyless.

The cloudy skies soon turned into a sunny day.

The tasteless supper was followed by a delicious dessert.

The bird flew under the fence and then over the house.

We live far from the school, but near the library.

The days are warm, but the nights are cool.

Tic-Tac-Toe

Play with a partner. Choose a tic-tac-toe board, and read aloud the word at the top. The first player marks an X in a space and writes a synonym for the word. The next player marks a space with an O and writes an antonym for the word. Play until someone gets three in a row.

happy

friendly

unusual

big

Assessment

Color the stars with antonyms red. Color the stars with synonyms blue. Then write a synonym for the word *happy* in one star. Write an antonym for *huge* in the other star.

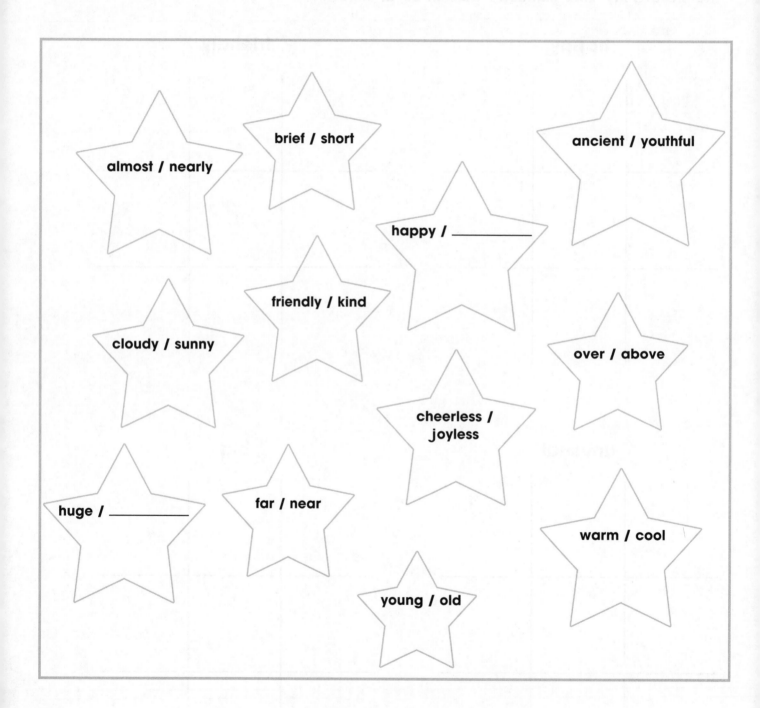

Overview   Multiple-Meaning Words

Directions and Sample Answers for Activity Pages

Day 1	See "Provide a Real-World Example" below.
Day 2	Read aloud the title and directions. Helps students read the sentences, focusing on the underlined words. Guide them to draw a line matching the sentences with the pictures.
Day 3	Read aloud the title and directions. Help students read each sentence and identify the homonym that correctly completes it. Help them write the word on the line. (ant, week, grate, knows, won, inn, hear, prey, peak, blew)
Day 4	Read aloud the title and directions. Help students cut out and glue words onto their Bingo cards. Cut out a set of words for yourself, fold them, and put them into a container. As you pick each word, use it in a sentence so students have context and know which word you are referring to. For example, you might say, "The number eight comes after seven."
Day 5	Read the directions aloud. Allow time for students to complete the first task. Then read aloud this sentence: *The girl sits on the stoop.* Have students draw a picture. Afterward, meet individually with students to discuss their results. Use their responses to plan further instruction and review.

Provide a Real-World Example

◆ **Ask:** *Where are my shoes?* After students point to your shoes, write **where** on chart paper. Then **say:** *I wear these shoes almost every day.* Write **wear** on the chart paper. **Say: Where** *and* **wear** *sound the same, but they have different spellings and meanings.* **Where** *and* **wear** *are homonyms.*

◆ Write this sentence on the board as you say it: *I wear these shoes because they wear well.* Point to the first **wear** in this sentence. Explain that it is a verb that means "to dress in something." Now point to the other **wear**. **Say:** *This* **wear** *is also a verb, but it means "to last long."* **Wear** *is a homograph, or a word that is spelled the same way but has different meanings depending on how we use it.*

◆ Hand out the Day 1 activity page. Read aloud the title and directions. Direct students to the first picture. **Say:** *This is a pear. We spell it* **p-e-a-r.** *The other pair, spelled* **p-a-i-r,** *means "two of something," such as a pair of socks. Draw a circle around the first pear. Repeat these steps for each picture, or if students are ready, they may work independently.*

Multiple-Meaning Words

where/wear

wear/wear

pear/pair

Picturing Homonyms

Draw a circle around the word that matches the picture.

pear   pair

route   root

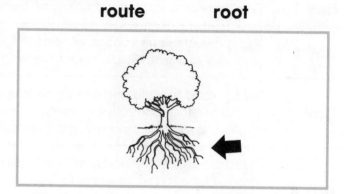

eight   ate

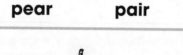

plain   plane

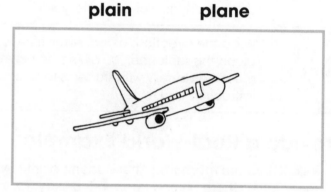

see   sea

meet   meat

sew   sow

flour   flower

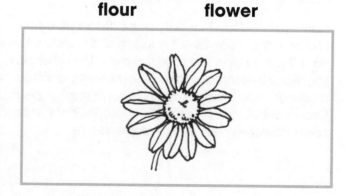

Homograph Make-a-Match

Read each sentence. Look at the underlined word. Draw a line from each sentence to the picture that shows the meaning of the underlined word.

The bird's <u>bill</u> is long.

I <u>plant</u> a seed.

The <u>dove</u> is beautiful.

He sits on the <u>stoop</u>.

He <u>tears</u> the paper.

He wears a <u>watch</u>.

I need a one-dollar <u>bill</u> to buy a ticket.

She <u>dove</u> into the water.

The <u>plant</u> is large.

I <u>stoop</u> to pick up a penny.

<u>Tears</u> roll down his cheek.

I <u>watch</u> through the window.

Circle It!

Read each sentence. Draw a circle around the homonym that completes the sentence. Write it on the line.

The _____ crawled on the rock.
         aunt   **ant**

There are seven days in a _____.
         weak   **week**

We _____ cheese to make pizza.
         grate   **great**

My teacher _____ everything!
         nose   **knows**

Who _____ the game?
         won   **one**

We are staying at the _____ for three nights.
         inn   **in**

Did you _____ the doorbell ring?
         hear   **here**

The fox ate its _____.
         pray   **prey**

The climbers reached the mountain's _____.
         peak   **peek**

The girl _____ out the candles.
         blew   **blue**

Homonym Bingo

Cut out the words. Select eight words and glue them onto your Bingo card.
Listen to your teacher use each word in a sentence. Make an X on the correct
homonym.
Three in a row wins **BINGO!**

	Free Space	

eight	ate	rain	rein	dye
die	by	buy	flea	flee
sees	seize	pier	peer	know
no	route	root	peek	seem
seam	raise	rays	peak	

Assessment

Draw a circle around the homonym that completes the sentence.

| Wear | Where | is the library?

The seeds the farmers | sow | sew | will grow into plants.

Steak is my favorite | meat | meet | .

The kite is | hi | high | in the sky.

Listen to your teacher. Draw a picture of what your teacher says.

Overview   Language Arts Content Words

Directions and Sample Answers for Activity Pages

Day 1	See "Provide a Real-World Example" below.
Day 2	Read aloud the title and directions. Helps students read the words in both columns and guide them to match the examples to their names.
Day 3	Read aloud the title and directions. Help students cut out the words and glue them in the correct part of the Venn diagram. Remind them to glue items that are fiction and nonfiction in the overlapping part. (**Fiction:** folktale, fairy tale, myth, plot, storybook; **Nonfiction**: essay, conclusion, newspaper, textbook, outline; **Both:** sentence, author, mystery, table of contents)
Day 4	Read aloud the title and directions. Help students read the clues and find answers in the word box. Model how to write a word into the crossword puzzle.
Day 5	Read the directions aloud. Allow time for students to complete the tasks. Afterward, meet individually with students to discuss their results. Use their responses to plan further instruction and review.

Provide a Real-World Example

◆ Display a book that you've recently read with the class. Write the words **book** and **title** on chart paper. Point to the title and **say:** *A title is the name of a book. What is the title of this book?* (Allow responses.) Then write **author** on the chart paper and **ask:** *Who is an author?* (Allow responses.) *An author is the person who writes a book. The author of this book is (author's name).* Write **illustrator** on the chart paper. Ask students what an illustrator is, and confirm that it is the person who draws the pictures. If the book on display is illustrated, encourage students to identify the illustrator's name. **Say:** *The title, author, and illustrator are on a book's front cover.* Write **front cover** on the chart paper. Turn the book over. Point to the words on the back cover. **Say:** *You can find a summary, or what a story is about, on the back cover. The summary is called a synopsis.* Write **back cover**, **summary**, and **synopsis** on the chart paper.

◆ **Say:** *True stories are nonfiction.* Write **nonfiction** on the chart paper. **Say:** *Stories that are not true are fiction.* Write **fiction** on the chart paper. **Ask:** *Is this book fiction or nonfiction?*

◆ Hand out the Day 1 activity page. Read aloud the title and directions. **Say:** *People read many different things in their day-to-day lives. We read some things for fun and others for information.* Read the first clue and the possible answers. **Say:** *We read the newspaper to find out what is happening in the world.* Guide students through the remaining clues.

English/Language Arts Content Words

book   back cover

title   summary

author   synopsis

illustrator   nonfiction

front cover   fiction

What We Read

Read the clue. Draw a circle around the answer.

We read it to find out what is happening in the world.

| newspaper | poem |

They often include a princess.

| signs | fairy tales |

Sometimes they rhyme, but they don't have to.

| letters | poems |

We read it to laugh.

| mystery | cartoon |

Young children enjoy reading these.

| storybooks | outlines |

They come in an envelope in our mailbox.

| letters | myths |

We read them to find out which way to go.

| rhymes | signs |

We read it for facts.

| textbook | storybook |

Match-Up

Draw a line to make a match.

ABCDEFG . . .   apostrophe

Roses are red.   exclamation point

Joe (runs) fast.   noun

Here is my (house.)   uppercase letters

Go team(!)   colon

Where are you(?)   verb

I'm your teacher.   comma

((2002–2012))   question mark

"Good morning."   parentheses

We've lived in three states(:)
New York, Ohio, and Florida.   alphabet

                                                 quotation marks

Dear Mr. Green,

We go to (West) (Ridge) (School).   period

Fiction, Nonfiction, or Both

Cut out the words. Glue each word under either "Fiction," "Nonfiction," or "Both."

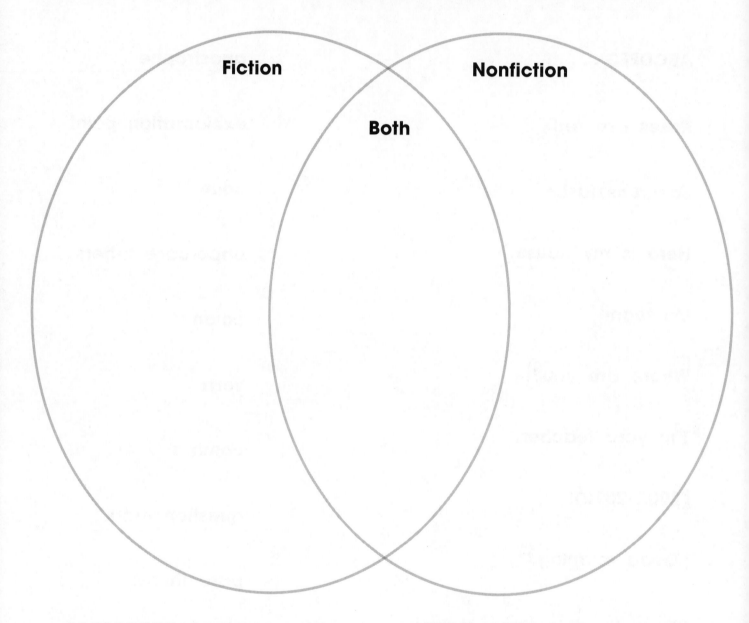

essay	sentence	conclusion	author
table of contents	folktale	textbook	fairy tale
myth	mystery	newspaper	outline
	plot	storybook	

Crossword Puzzle

Look at the clues. Find the words in the word box. Write the answers in the crossword puzzle.

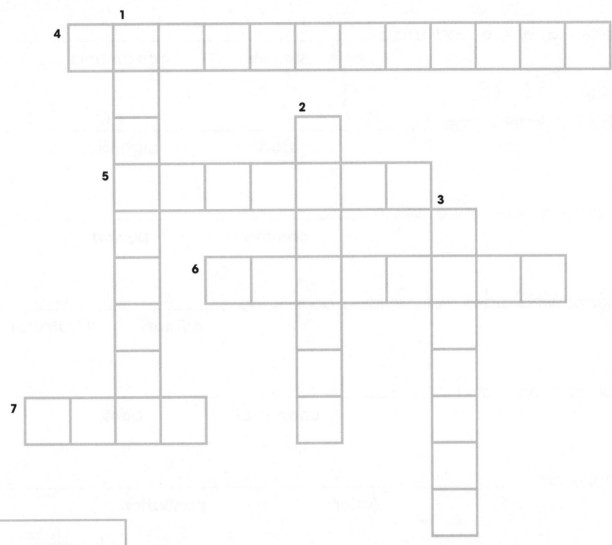

| cartoon |
| folktale |
| hero |
| introduction |
| newspaper |
| setting |
| villain |

Clues

Down

1. it has news reports
2. evil character
3. funny drawing

Across

4. the beginning part of a book
5. the time and place of a story
6. a story passed down through storytelling
7. brave character

Assessment

Read each sentence. Draw a circle around the correct word to complete each sentence. Write it on the line.

The letters **a**, **e**, **i**, **o**, and **u** are _____ .

        vowels   **consonants**

Z is the last letter in the _____ .

        story   **alphabet**

You can end a sentence with a _____ .

        comma   **period**

The person who draws pictures for a book is the _____ .

        author   **illustrator**

A villain is a type of a _____ .

        character   **book**

Fairy tales are _____ .

        fiction   **nonfiction**

Write the title, author, and main character of your favorite book on the lines below.

Title: _____

Author: _____

Main Character: _____

Overview   Government and Citizenship

Directions and Sample Answers for Activity Pages

Day 1	See "Provide a Real-World Example" below.
Day 2	Read aloud the title and directions. Help students read the sentences and answers. Guide them to circle the word that best completes each sentence and write it on the line.
Day 3	Read aloud the title and directions. Help students cut out and sort the words. Help them glue the words in the right column. (**Values:** honesty, responsibility; **Symbols:** bald eagle, Liberty Bell, U.S. flag; **Rights:** freedom, religion, speech, vote)
Day 4	Read aloud the title and directions. Read aloud the passage with students. Guide them to fill in the missing words with the words in the word box. Remind them to use context clues to help them. Tell them they may use each word only once.
Day 5	Read the directions aloud. Allow time for students to complete the tasks. Afterward, meet individually with students to discuss their results. Use their responses to plan further instruction and review.

Provide a Real-World Example

◆ Display a picture of the president. **Say:** *Who is this?* (Allow responses.) *This is the president of the United States. He is the leader of our country.* Write **president**, **United States of America**, and **leader** on chart paper. **Say:** *We choose, or vote for, the president and other government leaders. That's because we are a democracy, a government run by the people who live under it.* Write **vote**, **government**, and **democracy** on the chart paper.

◆ Hand out the Day 1 activity page. Read aloud the title and directions. **Say:** *Our government has three branches: legislative, executive, and judicial.* Direct students' attention to the "Legislative Branch" column. **Say:** *The legislative branch makes the laws. Congress is part of the legislative branch.* Write **Congress** under "Legislative Branch." *Congress is made up of two parts, the House of Representatives and the Senate. Let's write those words under "Legislative Branch," too.*

◆ Direct students to the "Executive Branch" column. **Say:** *The president and vice president are parts of the executive branch. Their job is to make sure people follow the laws. A group of officials known as the Cabinet help the president. They are part of the executive branch, too.* Guide students to write **president**, **vice president**, and **Cabinet** under "Executive Branch." Now focus the class on the "Judicial Branch" column. **Say:** *The judicial branch includes the courts. The courts help people when there are questions about the laws. The highest court is the Supreme Court, which includes nine judges. Let's write* **courts**, ***Supreme Court**, and* **judges** *under "Judicial Branch."*

Government and Citizenship Words

president

United States of America

leader

vote

government

democracy

Branches of the U.S. Government

Write the words for each branch of government on the lines beneath that branch.

Cabinet	Congress	courts	House of Representatives
president	judges	Senate	Supreme Court vice president

Legislative Branch   **Executive Branch**   **Judicial Branch**

_____   _____   _____

_____   _____   _____

_____   _____   _____

Complete-a-Sentence

Read each sentence. Draw a circle around the correct word or words that complete each sentence. Write the word or words on the line.

The _____ is a national bird and
bald eagle   pigeon
symbol for the United States.

The _____, a symbol of freedom,
Liberty Bell   volunteer
is on display in Philadelphia.

If you are born in the United States, you are an American

_____.
leader   citizen

As an American citizen, it is your _____
power   duty
to follow the laws of the land.

Judges are part of the _____ branch.
executive   judicial

The first U.S. _____ had 13 stars for the
flag   liberty bell
13 colonies.

The song "The Star-Spangled Banner" is America's

_____.
national anthem   pledge of allegiance

Sort It Out, America!

Cut out the words. Glue each word under "Values," "Symbols," or "Rights."

Values	Symbols	Rights

bald eagle	freedom	honesty	Liberty Bell	religion
responsibility	speech	U.S. flag	vote	

Good Citizens

Read the passage. Find the missing words in the word box. Write them on the lines.

citizens	community	laws
respect	rules	Volunteers

Good _____ try to make the world a better place.

Good citizens care about their families and their friends. They treat their

family and friends with _____. Good citizens make their

_____ a better place to live. _____ are

good citizens because they give their time to help others. Good citizens

follow _____ at home and at school. They also follow

rules of their community. These rules are called _____.

Laws keep people safe.

Assessment

Read the questions. Draw a circle around the answer.

Which branch of government makes the laws?

judicial   **executive**   **legislative**

Who is the leader of the executive branch?

vice president   **president**   **senator**

Which is NOT a symbol for America?

judge   **bald eagle**   **Liberty Bell**

Who votes to elect the president?

vice president only   **American citizens**   **senators only**

What do you call rules of a community?

national anthem   **rights**   **laws**

Draw and label a symbol of the United States of America.

_____

Overview Geography

Directions and Sample Answers for Activity Pages

Day 1	See "Provide a Real-World Example" below.
Day 2	Read aloud the title and directions. Help students find the word that correctly completes each sentence and write it on the line. (compass rose, legend, map, scale, symbol, globe)
Day 3	Read aloud the title and directions. Help students cut out and sort the words. Help them glue the words in the right columns. (**Country:** Israel, Spain, United States; **State:** New York, Oregon, South Dakota; **Ocean:** Atlantic, Indian, Pacific)
Day 4	Read aloud the title and directions. Help students draw the route on their map, circle the destination, and write it on the line. As an extra challenge, encourage students to create routes for a partner to follow on the map. (home)
Day 5	Read the directions aloud. Allow time for students to complete the tasks. Afterward, meet individually with students to discuss their results. Use their responses to plan further instruction and review.

Provide a Real-World Example

◆ Display several maps, such as a town map, a U.S. map, and a world map. Write **map** on chart paper. **Ask:** *How are these maps alike?* (Allow responses.) *All of these maps show locations of places. They all include a compass rose, which shows which way is north, south, east, and west.* Write **compass rose**, **north**, **south**, **east**, and **west** on chart paper. *All of the maps have a key, or legend, that tells what the different symbols on the map mean, such as forests and rivers.* Write **key**, **legend**, **symbols**, **forests**, and **rivers** on the chart paper. Point to a scale on one of the maps. **Say:** *Most maps have a scale to measure and compare distances. It shows the distance between places on a smaller scale. For example, one inch on a map might be 100 miles in the real world.* Write **scale** on the chart paper.

◆ **Ask:** *How are these maps different?* (Allow responses.) *Each map shows different geographical features. The town map shows details about a neighborhood, such as street names and where places are located, including the hospital, park, school, museum, etc.* Write these places on the chart paper. Explain that a state map shows where states are located and geographical features such as lakes, prairies, and plains. Write these words on the chart paper. **Say:** *A world map shows global features, such as location of countries and oceans.* Write these words on the chart paper, too.

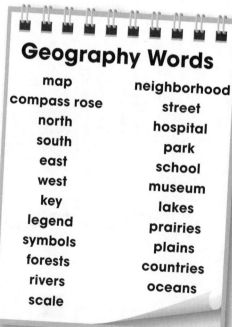

Geography Words

map	neighborhood
compass rose	street
north	hospital
south	park
east	school
west	museum
key	lakes
legend	prairies
symbols	plains
forests	countries
rivers	oceans
scale	

◆ Hand out the Day 1 activity page. Guide students to match the geographical pictures on the left side with the words on the right side. Model the first example. **Say:** *This symbol is on every map. It shows which way is north, south, east, and west. It is called a compass rose. Let's draw a line to the words* **compass rose.** Continue to model as needed.

Geography Match-Up!

Draw a line to match the pictures to the words.

scale

railroad symbol

map

legend

hospital symbol

globe

river symbol

compass rose

Complete-a-Sentence

Read each sentence. Find the missing word in the word box. Write it on the line.

compass rose	globe	legend
map	scale	symbol

A _____ shows where north, south, east, and west are on a map.

To find out what symbols on a map mean, look at a _____.

A _____ is a special drawing that shows information about an area.

"1 inch equals 100 miles" is something you might see on a map's _____.

A small drawing of a pine tree is a _____ for a forest on a map.

You can see all of the countries on a _____.

Country, State, or Ocean?

Cut out the words. Glue each word under "Country," "State," or "Ocean."

Country	State	Ocean

Atlantic	**Israel**	**Indian**	**New York**	**Oregon**
Pacific	**South Dakota**	**Spain**	**United States**	

Name _____

Hillside Map

Read the directions. Draw a line to follow the route. Circle the end location. Write the end location on the line.

Directions

Start at the park. Go two blocks north on Oak Street. Go east one block on Green Street. Go north one block on Elm Street. Go east one and a half blocks on Grove Street. Where are you? Write your answer on the line below.

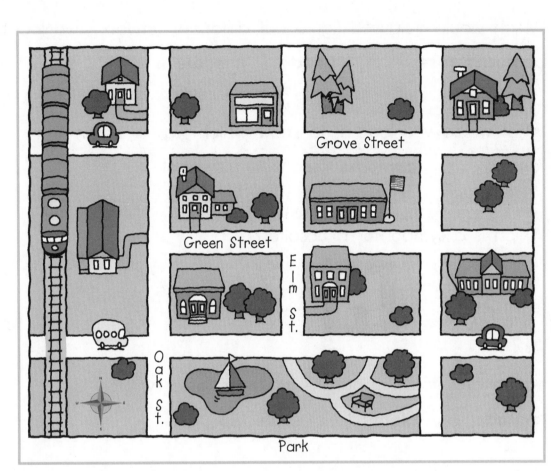

_____

Extra Challenge

As an extra challenge, write a new route for a partner to follow.

_____   _____

_____   _____

_____   _____

_____   _____

Assessment

Read the questions. Draw a circle around the answer.

Which would help you figure out distance between two locations?

compass rose   **legend**   **scale**

What would you look at to know which way is west?

legend   **compass rose**   **symbol**

Which is a symbol for a hospital?

Where can you find out the meaning of a symbol?

legend   **globe**   **scale**

Draw a map of the inside of your school. Include a compass rose and a legend.

Overview   Communities

Directions and Sample Answers for Activity Pages

Day 1	See "Provide a Real-World Example" below.
Day 2	Read aloud the title and directions. Help students cut out the words and glue each one in the correct part of the Venn diagram. Remind them to glue items that are both rural and suburban in the overlapping part. (**Rural:** far from city, farms, ranches; **Suburban:** near a city, shopping malls, travel to city for job; **Both:** live in houses)
Day 3	Read aloud the title and directions. Help students read the passage and the questions. Encourage them to return to the text to find the answers. Then guide them to draw a circle around the correct answers. (skyscraper, anywhere, apartment buildings, Tokyo, stores, bus)
Day 4	Read aloud the title and directions. Help students find the word that correctly completes each sentence and write it on the line. (colony, Pilgrims, houses, food, community, girls, boys, crops, goods, meeting house)
Day 5	Read the directions aloud. Allow time for students to complete the tasks. Afterward, meet individually with students to discuss their results. Use their responses to plan further instruction and review.

Provide a Real-World Example

◆ Ask students what comes to mind when they think of a community. Write down their ideas on chart paper. After they brainstorm, **say:** *(name of your community) is your community. You live here and go to school here. You and your parents shop in the stores and use the banks in your community. You ride your bicycle in the park and play with friends at the playground, borrow books from the library, and see movies at the movie theater. You visit the doctor each year, and maybe you've even had to go to the hospital.* Write the following on chart paper: **community**, **stores**, **bank**, **park**, **playground**, **library**, **movie theater**, **hospital**.

◆ **Ask:** *What else do you do in your community?* Add their responses to the chart paper.

◆ Hand out the Day 1 activity page. **Say:** *A community is a place where people live, work, and play. Let's look at the words in the word box and sort them in the "Live," "Work," or "Play" columns.* Provide an example. **Say:** *A tenement is an apartment building. Some people in cities live in tenements. People lived in tenements long ago, too. Let's write* **tenements** *under "Live."* Then **say:** *A governor is a person who runs a community. He or she works for the community. Let's write* **governor** *under "Work." A colony is a territory or community settled by people from a particular country. The first communities in our country were colonies. Let's write* **colony** *under "Live," too.* Continue in this way with each word. If the word has to do with communities long ago, point that out to students.

Community Words

community

stores

bank

park

playground

library

movie theater

hospital

Name _____

Live, Work, Play

Look at the words in the word box. Write each word under "Live," "Work," or "Play." Some may work under more than one heading.

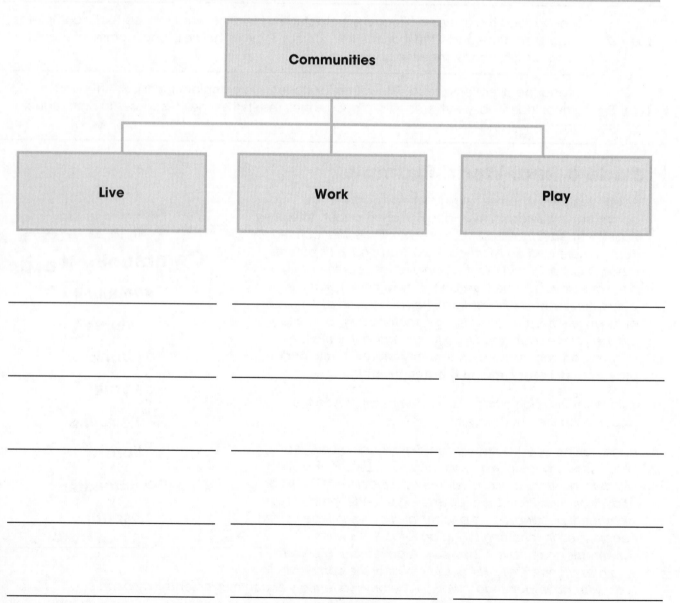

colony	governor	house	library
market	merchant	miners	movie theater
office building	park	playground	school
shipping port	skyscraper	tenement	zoo

Communities

Live   **Work**   **Play**

 Unit 11 • Everyday Vocabulary Intervention Activities Grade 3 • ©2011 Newmark Learning, LLC

Rural and Suburban Communities

Read the passages. Cut out the words. Glue each word in either "Rural," "Suburban," or "Both."

Rural Communities

A rural community is far from a city. Many people live and work in a rural community. A rural community often has farms and ranches. Farmers grow crops in their fields. Ranchers raise animals. People in rural communities live in houses.

Suburban Communities

A suburban community is near a city. Many people live and work in a suburban community. Some people travel to the city for their jobs. A suburban community has more people than a rural community. Most suburban communities have shopping malls with many stores in one place. People drive cars in a suburban community. People in the suburbs live in houses.

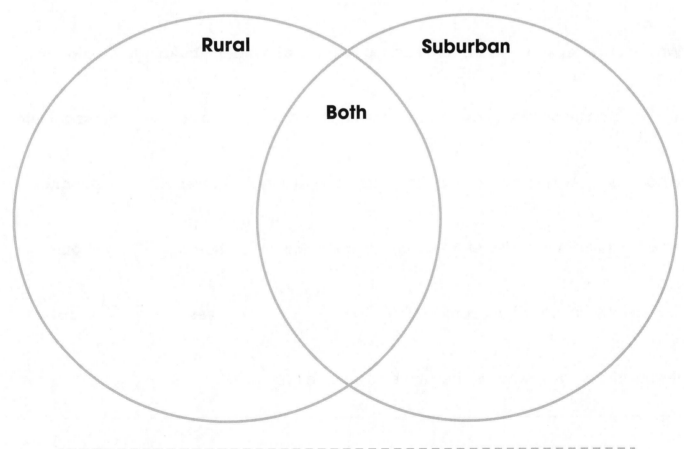

far from city	farms	travel to city for job	near a city
ranches	shopping malls	live in houses	

Urban Communities

Read the story. Answer the questions below by circling the correct word or words.

An urban community is in a city. An urban community is the largest type of community. The people who live in urban communities come from around the world. Tokyo and New York City are two examples of urban communities.

An urban community has many tall buildings, or skyscrapers. Some are apartment buildings where people live. Other buildings are offices where people work. An urban community has many stores. People buy food, clothing, books, and more in the stores. How do people get around urban communities? They travel on trains, buses, and subways.

Which would you see in an urban community?   **skyscraper**   **ranch**

Where are people in urban communities from?   **anywhere**   **farms**

Where do people in urban communities live?   **apartment buildings**   **stores**

Which is an example of an urban community?   **Tokyo**   **Pleasantville**

What can you find many of in an urban community?   **stores**   **beaches**

How might someone travel in an urban community?   **horse**   **bus**

Do you live in an urban community?   **yes**   **no**

If you circled yes, what is the name of your city?

_____

If you circled no, what city is close to where you live?

_____

Plymouth: One of America's First Communities

Read the passage. Then complete the sentences using words from the word box.

One of the first colonies, or communities, in America was Plymouth, Massachusetts. Plymouth was settled by the Pilgrims, English people who came here for religious freedom. The Pilgrims built their own houses. They grew their own food. They made their clothes and other things such as candles and soap. Many families were large. Every child worked. Girls helped cook, sew, and take care of small children. Boys fished and hunted. Both boys and girls took care of the farm animals. Children did not go to school. Their parents taught them to read.

The colonists grew corn and other crops. They also traded goods. They sent fur, fish, and wood to England. They made all kinds of goods that they traded among themselves.

The first colonists all lived and worked near one another. They helped one another with different chores. And they attended church together. The meeting house was important to the whole community. It was used as a church and as a place to talk over community business.

boys	colony	community	crops	food
girls	goods	houses	meeting house	Pilgrims

A _____ is a community settled by people from another country.

The _____ came to Plymouth from England.

The Pilgrims built their own _____ and grew their own _____.

Everyone in the _____ worked, even the children.

The _____ helped cook and sew, while the _____ fished and hunted.

Corn is one of the _____ the colonists grew.

Fur, fish, and wood are examples of _____ the colonists traded.

The colonists went to church and discussed community business in the _____.

Assessment

Cut out the words. Glue each word under "Rural," "Suburban," or "Urban."

Rural	Suburban	Urban

Identify which type of community you live in. Draw a picture.

city	crops	farm	house
shopping mall	skyscraper	rancher	subway

Overview Communication and Technology

Directions and Sample Answers for Activity Pages

Day 1	See "Provide a Real-World Example" below.
Day 2	Read aloud the title and directions. Help students read the passage. Then help them cut out the words and phrases, sort them, and glue them in the correct columns. (**Wheel:** cart, over 5,000 years old, used to shape clay; **Steam Engine:** powered by heating water, steamboat, steam locomotive; **Internal Combustion:** airplane, car, powered by burning fuel)
Day 3	Read aloud the title and directions. Help students read the passage and the questions. Encourage them to return to the text to find the answers. Then guide them to draw a circle around the correct answers. (phonograph, record player, radio, phonograph, Marconi, enjoy music)
Day 4	Read aloud the title and directions. Divide the class into small groups to play charades. Instruct each small group to cut out the words and put them into a cup or a hat. Model how to play.
Day 5	Read the directions aloud. Allow time for students to complete the task. Afterward, meet individually with students to discuss their results. Use their responses to plan further instruction and review.

Provide a Real-World Example

◆ **Say:** *This morning, my alarm clock woke me up. I turned on the coffee maker and watched the news on TV. I checked my e-mail and finally hopped into my car and drove to school.* On chart paper, write **alarm clock**, **coffee maker**, **television**, **e-mail**, and **car**. Read the list and **say:** *What types of technology did you use this morning?* Add students' responses to the list.

◆ **Say:** *We use technology all the time. From e-mail to airplanes, new forms of technology and communication make our lives easier.* Write **technology** and **communication** on the chart paper. **Say:** *Long ago, many of the things we use today had not yet been invented. People communicated by mail and walked or rode horses to get places.* Encourage a discussion of what life must have been like before today's technology.

◆ Hand out the Day 1 activity page. Read aloud the title and directions. **Say:** *People used candles for light long ago. I will write **candle** on the "Long Ago" side. Today, people use lamps. Let's write **lamp** on the "Today" side. We ride in cars today to go to places. Let's write **car** on the "Today" side. Long ago, people rode in carriages pulled by horses. Let's write **horse and carriage** on the "Long Ago" side.* Continue in this way with each of the words in the word box.

Communication and Technology Words

alarm clock

coffee maker

television

e-mail

car

technology

communication

Technology Today and Long Ago

Look at the words in the word box. Write each word under "Today" or "Long Ago."

airplane	broom	candle	car
computer	horse and carriage	lamp	oven
steamship	telegraph	vacuum	cell phone

Today	Long Ago

Inventions on the Move

Read the passage. Then cut out the words and phrases and glue them under "Wheel," "Steam Engine," or "Internal Combustion."

What is one of the most important inventions of all time? Believe it or not, it's the wheel! Invented more than 5,000 years ago, the first wheel was used by potters to shape clay. Around the same time, heavy wooden wheels were used on carts to move big objects. Today we find wheels everywhere, from school buses to space shuttles.

Another important invention was the steam engine. A steam engine uses heated water to create power. In 1770, people rode in the world's first passenger steamboat. Shortly after, in 1804, the first steam locomotive, or train, was invented.

The invention of the internal combustion engine brought transportation into a new era. Inside the engine, fuel burns, or combusts, to produce power. The internal combustion engine led to the invention of the first car and, after, the first airplane.

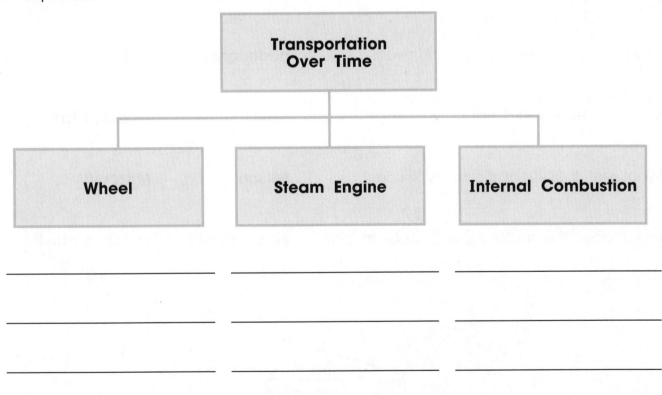

The Modernizing of Music

Read the story. Answer the questions below by circling the correct word or words.

Technology makes work easier. Technology also makes it easier to have fun. From the invention of recorded sound to today's high-tech sound systems, technology has made it possible for people to enjoy music. The very first record player, called a phonograph, was invented by Thomas Edison in 1877. It allowed people to listen to recorded sounds for the first time. The radio was another invention that made it easier for people to enjoy music. Guglielmo Marconi, inventor of the radio, began by sending radio signals short distances. He made history when he sent the first radio transmissions across the Atlantic Ocean in 1901.

Which invention plays music?	**phonograph**	**telegraph**
What is a phonograph?	**record player**	**telephone**
Which did Guglielmo Marconi invent?	**phonograph**	**radio**
Which was invented first?	**radio**	**phonograph**
Who sent the first radio transmissions?	**Edison**	**Marconi**
What does the radio allow people to do?	**enjoy music**	**watch a movie**

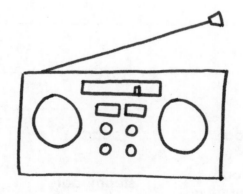

Charades

Cut out the words. Fold them and put them in a cup or hat. Pick one. Identify yourself as transportation, communication, or entertainment. You may use words to describe what you are, but not the word itself. The player that guesses correctly goes next.

bicycle	bridge	bus	canal	car
cell phone	computer	e-mail	motorcycle	MP3 player
radio	road	skateboard	train	steamship
steam engine	telegraph	telephone	television	

Assessment

Read the questions. Write your answers on the lines.

What products did you use to communicate in the past week? Make a list.

_____

_____

_____

What type of transportation did you use in the past week? Make a list.

_____

_____

_____

What technology did you use to have fun in the past week? Make a list.

_____

_____

_____

Overview Life Science: Plant and Animal Habitats

Directions and Sample Answers for Activity Pages

Day 1	See "Provide a Real-World Example" below.
Day 2	Read aloud the title and directions. Help students find the word that correctly completes each sentence and write it on the line. (shelter, habitat, adapt, homes, weather, change, hide, survive)
Day 3	Read aloud the title and directions. Help students read the passage. Then help them cut out the words. Guide students to identify the four layers of the rain forest and glue them in the right place. Then help them glue the words for the plants and animals that live in each layer.
Day 4	Read aloud the title and directions. Help students identify each word as associated with a polar or a desert habitat and write it under the correct place on the pedestal chart. (**Polar:** Arctic, cold, hibernate, penguin, polar bear, snow and ice; **Desert:** cactus, camel, hot, sandy, snake, oasis)
Day 5	Read the directions aloud. Allow time for students to complete the task. Afterward, meet individually with students to discuss their results. Use their responses to plan further instruction and review.

Provide a Real-World Example

◆ **Ask:** *What do you need to live, or survive?* Write students' ideas on chart paper. Then **say:** *You need oxygen to breathe. You need food for energy and to stay healthy. You need water to stay hydrated. And you need shelter to stay warm and safe.* Write **need**, **survive**, **oxygen**, **food**, **energy**, **water**, and **shelter** on chart paper.

◆ Direct students' attention to a plant in the classroom or a plant outside. **Say:** *Plants are like people. They also need certain things to survive. Some of those needs are the same and some are different. What do you think a plant needs?* (Allow responses.) Write their ideas on the chart paper. Then **say:** *Plants need sunlight. Leaves use the sunlight to make food. The food helps the plant grow. Some plants need very little water, but most plants need at least some water to live. Plants also need soil. Soil has nutrients and minerals that help the plant grow. It's like food for plants.* Write **sunlight**, **soil**, **nutrients**, and **minerals** on the chart paper.

◆ Hand out the Day 1 activity page. Read aloud the title and directions. **Say:** *Every living thing—plants and animals—has basic needs to survive. Both animals and plants need water. Let's write **water** in the overlapping section. Plants need soil to survive, but animals do not. Let's write **soil** in the "Plant" section. Animals need food to survive. Let's write **food** in the "Animal" section.* Continue in this way with each of the words in the word box.

Life Science Words

need	shelter
survive	sunlight
oxygen	soil
food	nutrients
energy	minerals
water	

Name _____

Plant and Animal Needs

Look at the words in the word box. Write each word in "Animal," "Plant," or "Both."

water	soil	food	nutrients
oxygen	shelter	space	sunlight

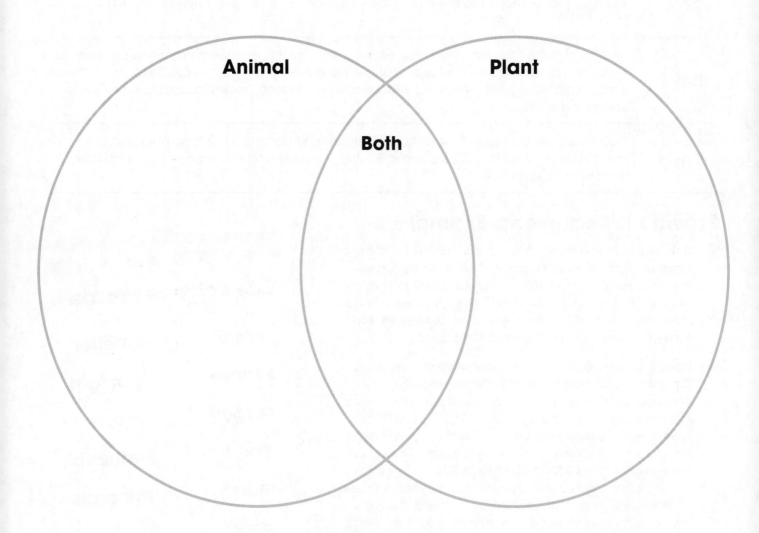

Animal   **Plant**

Both

Animal Adaptations

Read the passage. Use the words in the word box to complete each sentence. Write the words on the line.

A habitat is a place in nature that has the food, water, and shelter an animal needs to live. Animals depend on their habitats for survival. But a habitat is only part of what helps animals survive. Over millions of years, animals have adapted, or changed so that they can survive in their habitats. Animals have changed their bodies or how they move so they can get food, build homes, survive extreme weather, and attract mates. The changes that let animals survive are called adaptations.

There are many kinds of adaptations. The shape of a bird's beak is an adaptation that helps it get food. Being able to live in trees is an adaptation that protects animals from enemies on the ground. Camouflage, or changing color, allows animals to hide from an enemy or to capture prey.

adapt	change	habitat	homes
hide	shelter	survive	weather

To survive, an animal needs food, water, and _____.

A _____ is where animals live and have their needs met.

To survive in their habitat, sometimes animals must change, or

_____.

Some adaptations help animals build _____ and survive

extreme _____.

Camouflage is the ability of an animal to _____ color.

Camouflage helps animals _____ from their enemies.

Adaptations help animals _____.

Living in the Rain Forest

Read the passage. Cut out the words. Label the rain forest parts by gluing the layer names in the correct spots. Then glue the words for the plants and animals that live in each layer.

A tropical rain forest has four layers. The bottom layer is the forest floor. Woody vines grow from the forest floor. Insects have nests on the forest floors. The second layer is the understory. Jaguars rest or hide in the understory. Tree frogs live there, too. The third layer is the canopy. More animals live in the canopy layer than any other layer, including butterflies, bats, and sloths. Fruits grow in the canopy layer. The top of the rain forest is the emergent layer. It is home to many birds, such as toucans, parrots, and macaws. Orchids live in the emergent layer. Orchids do not need soil and can live on the branches.

bats	butterflies	canopy	emergent layer	forest floor
fruit	insects	jaguars	macaws	parrots
sloths	toucans	tree frogs	understory	woody vines

Polar Opposite Habitats

Look at the words in the word box. Write each word under "Polar" or "Desert."

Arctic	cactus	camel	cold	hibernate	hot
penguin	polar bear	sandy	snake	snow and ice	oasis

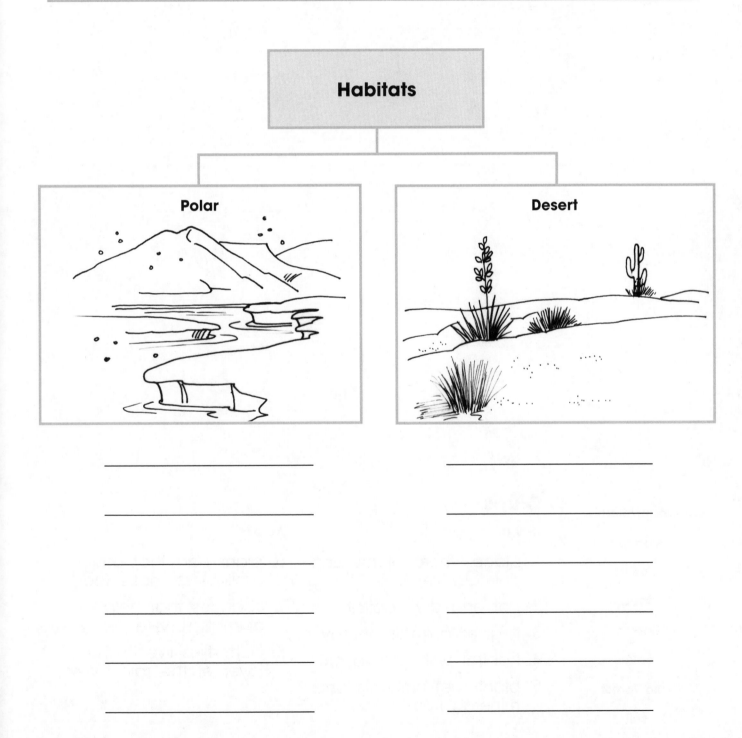

Habitats

Polar

Desert

_____   _____

_____   _____

_____   _____

_____   _____

_____   _____

Assessment

Look at the clues. Find the words in the word box. Write the answers in the crossword puzzle.

Clues

Down

1. place where plants and animals live
2. hot and dry habitat
3. it gives animals energy
4. habitat with four layers
5. plants get nutrients and minerals from it

Across

6. plant part that uses sunlight to make food
7. changes that help animals survive
8. butterflies live in this layer of the rain forest

Word Box:
adaptations
canopy
desert
food
habitat
leaves
rain forest
soil

Overview   Life Science: Plant and Animal Life Cycles

Directions and Sample Answers for Activity Pages

Day 1	See "Provide a Real-World Example" below.
Day 2	Read aloud the title and directions. Help students read the sentences and answers. Guide them to draw a circle around the word or words that correctly complete each sentence and write the word or words on the line. (seed, three, cotyledon, embryo, seed coat, trunk, photosynthesis, carbon dioxide, gas, sun, sugar, oxygen)
Day 3	Read aloud the title and directions. Help students read the passage. Then guide them as they cut out the words and glue them in the order of the life cycle. (egg, caterpillar, pupa, butterfly)
Day 4	Read aloud the title and directions. Help students read the passage and the questions. Encourage them to return to the text to find the answers. Then guide them to draw a circle around the correct answers. (reproduction, stamen, pistil, pollen, wind, seeds)
Day 5	Read the directions aloud. Allow time for students to complete the task. Afterward, meet individually with students to discuss their results. Use their responses to plan further instruction and review.

Provide a Real-World Example

◆ Display pictures of people at various ages, from newborn to elderly. **Ask:** *How are you different from a baby?* (Allow responses.) *How are you different from a grown-up? How are you different from an elderly person?* (Allow responses.) Then **say:** *All living things grow. Living things include animals and plants. Living things change as they grow. All living things have a life cycle. A life cycle is the order in which living things change.* Write **animals, plants, grow, change,** and **life cycle** on chart paper.

◆ **Say:** *Many animals begin their life cycles as eggs. Animals grow during their life cycles. Think about how you've grown since you were a newborn baby. Think about how you will continue to grow in years to come. Animals die at the end of the life cycle.* Write **eggs** and **die** on the chart paper. Then **say:** *Plants have life cycles, too. They begin their lives as seeds, not eggs.* Write **seeds** on the chart paper. Then tell students that this week they will explore words having to do with animal and plant life cycles.

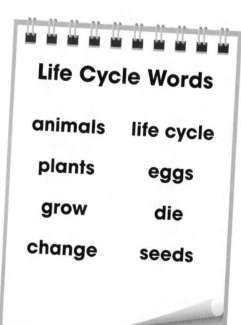

Life Cycle Words

animals   life cycle

plants   eggs

grow   die

change   seeds

◆ Hand out the Day 1 activity page. Read aloud the title and directions. Remind students that in a Venn diagram, we put items that have to do with both categories in the overlapping section. **Say:** *All living things, plants and animals, have a life cycle.* Write **life cycle** in the overlapping part. Now point out the word **root**. **Say:** *The root is the part of the plant that grows underground. A tree root holds the tree in the ground.* **Root** *is a plant word.* Write **root** in the "Plant" section. Now look at the word **egg**. *Many animals begin their lives as an egg.* Write **egg** in the "Animal" section. Continue in this way with each of the words in the word box.

Plant, Animal, or Both?

Look at the words in the word box. Write each word in "Animal," "Plant," or "Both."

adult	caterpillar	die	egg	embryo
life cycle	newborn	photosynthesis	pupa	root
seed coat	tadpole	tree		

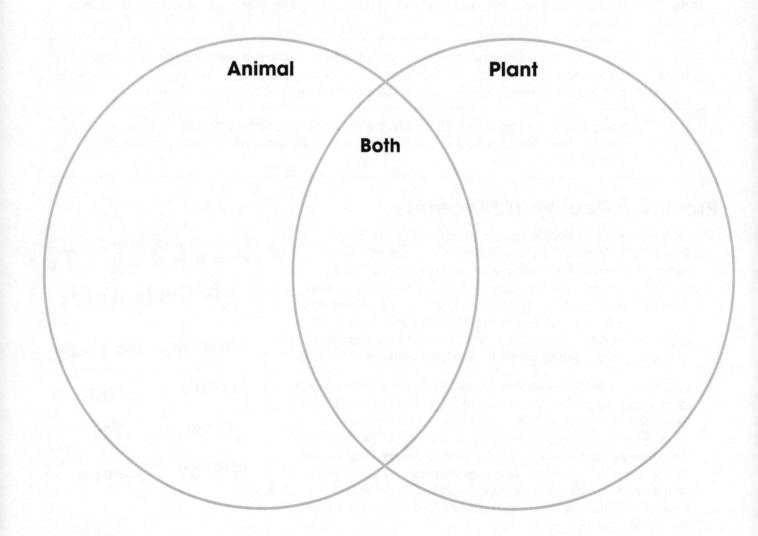

What a Tree Needs

Read each sentence. Draw a circle around the correct word or words that complete each sentence. Write it on the line.

The life cycle of a tree begins with a seed. Seeds have three parts: embryo, cotyledon, and seed coat. The embryo is the baby tree within the seed. The cotyledon is the tree's first food source. It looks like tiny leaves. The seed coat protects the embryo. When a tree starts to grow, a stem pushes up from the ground. All plants have stems. A tree's stem is called a trunk. The trunk is covered with bark. The bark protects the trunk.

A tree needs air, water, and soil to grow. A growing plant also needs light. Sunlight helps the tree make its own food. This process is called photosynthesis. First, leaves take in a gas called carbon dioxide through tiny holes. Tree roots take in water from the soil. The water goes up the trunk and into the leaves. The light for photosynthesis comes from the sun. Inside the leaves, the carbon dioxide, water, and light combine to make sugar that a tree uses for food. After photosynthesis, oxygen is released into the air.

The life cycle of a tree begins with a _____.

                              root   **seed**

All seeds have _____ parts.

                    two   **three**

A baby tree is the _____.

                    embryo   **seed coat**

The _____ looks like tiny leaves.

           cotyledon   **embryo**

The _____ protects the embryo.

            bark   **seed coat**

Bark protects the _____.

                    embryo   **trunk**

_____ is the process trees go through to make food.

Oxygen   **Photosynthesis**

Trees take in _____ through holes in their leaves.

          carbon dioxide   **water**

Carbon dioxide is a _____.

                liquid   **gas**

The _____ provides light for photosynthesis.

        sun   **ocean**

Water, light, and carbon dioxide combine to make _____.

                  sugar   **an egg**

Photosynthesis ends with the release of _____ into the air.

            pollen   **oxygen**

Butterfly Life Cycle

Read the passage. Cut out the words. Glue them in order, starting at the top.

A butterfly begins its life as a tiny egg. When the egg hatches, a caterpillar comes out. The caterpillar eats and eats. It gets very big! Soon, the caterpillar sheds its skin. Next, the caterpillar grows a hard shell and becomes a pupa. Inside the hard case, the caterpillar changes. It grows wings. Finally, the butterfly comes out of the pupa. Now the butterfly can lay eggs. The life cycle starts again.

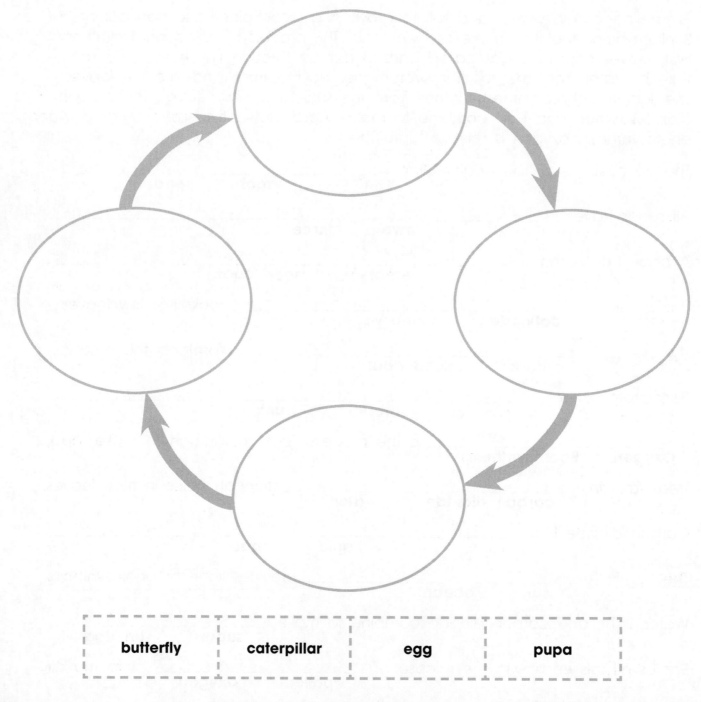

| **butterfly** | **caterpillar** | **egg** | **pupa** |

Plant Reproduction

Read the passage. Answer the questions below by drawing a circle around the correct word.

Plants reproduce, or make new plants. Flowers have three main parts that make reproduction happen: the pistil, the stamen, and the petals. The stamen is the male part of the plant that makes pollen. The pistil is the female part of the plant that makes eggs. Pollination is the moving of pollen, which has the male cells, from the stamen to the pistil. This process fertilizes the eggs.

Wind, water, and insects move the pollen from the stamen to the pistil. Fertilized eggs make seeds. The seeds can grow into new plants. The seeds fall from the plant and the plant's life cycle is complete.

What is it called when plants make new plants?	**reproduction**	**pollination**
Which is a male part of a plant?	**pistil**	**stamen**
Which part of a plant makes eggs?	**pistil**	**stamen**
What fertilizes the plant's eggs?	**pollen**	**petals**
Which can move pollen?	**wind**	**snow**
Fertilized eggs make what?	**stamen**	**seeds**

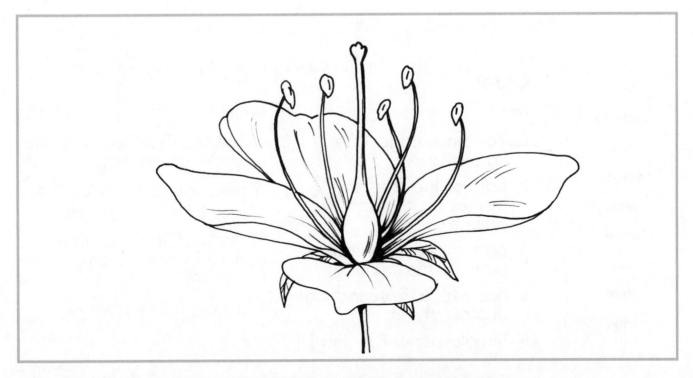

Assessment

Look at the clues. Find the words in the word box. Write the answers in the crossword puzzle.

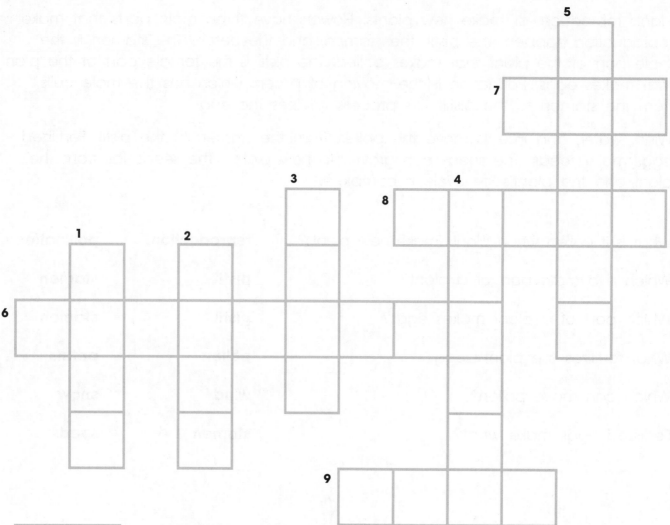

bark
butterfly
die
oxygen
pistil
pupa
roots
stem
wind

Clues

Down

1. life cycle stage after caterpillar
2. part of the tree that pushes up through the ground
3. part of the tree that protects the trunk
4. gas that is released after photosynthesis
5. female part of a plant

Across

6. animal that begins its life cycle as an egg
7. what animals do at the end of their life cycle
8. parts of the tree that take in water from the soil
9. it can move pollen

Overview Earth Science

Directions and Sample Answers for Activity Pages

Day 1	See "Provide a Real-World Example" below.
Day 2	Read aloud the title and directions. Help students cut out the words and phrases, sort them, and glue them in the correct part of the pedestal chart. (**Earth:** planet, has oxygen, orbits the sun; **Sun:** star, center of solar system, produces light; **Moon:** satellite, craters, crescent)
Day 3	Read aloud the title and directions. Help students read the passage. Guide them as they cut out the words and glue them in the order of the water cycle. (evaporation, condensation, precipitation, runoff)
Day 4	Read aloud the title and directions. Help students find the word or words that correctly complete each sentence and write the word or words on the line. (layers, crust, ocean floor, plates, fault, earthquake, crash)
Day 5	Read the directions aloud. Allow time for students to complete the task. Afterward, meet individually with students to discuss their results. Use their responses to plan further instruction and review.

Provide a Real-World Example

◆ Put a rock on display. Invite a volunteer to hold the rock. **Ask:** *How does the rock feel? Is it hard or soft?* After the student responds, **say:** *Rocks can be very powerful. A rock rolling down a hill can crush things. Now think of raindrops falling on the ground. Which do you think is more powerful, rocks or raindrops?* (Allow responses.) Then **say:** *Raindrops may not be able to crush things. But, over time, they can wear away rock and even shape Earth! When raindrops hit the ground, they break loose tiny bits of rock and dirt. As the raindrops move, they carry the tiny bits along with them. Slowly, the bits of rock and dirt wear away Earth's surface. This is called erosion. Wind, ice, and sand also cause erosion. Harmless little raindrops, then, are just as powerful as big rocks.* Write **rocks, Earth, raindrops, dirt, erosion, wind, ice,** and **sand** on chart paper.

Earth Science Words

rocks   erosion

Earth   wind

raindrops   ice

dirt   sand

◆ Remind students that Earth science is the study of Earth and space. Explain that this week they will explore Earth science words.

◆ Hand out the Day 1 activity page. Read aloud the title and directions. **Say:** *Earth is called the Blue Planet because of all the water on its surface. I'll draw a line from* **Earth** *to* **Blue Planet.** Draw attention to the next word, **sun.** **Say:** *I know that the sun is a star. Let's draw a line from* **sun** *to* **star.** Continue to match the words in the columns.

Solar System Match-Up

Draw a line to match the words in the left column with the words in the right column.

Earth	slow-moving chunk of ice
sun	Blue Planet
crust	Earth's surface
erosion	plant or animal remains
evaporation	star
fossil	sun and planets
glacier	water changing to gas
solar system	wearing away of Earth
volcano	mountain created by lava

Exploring the Solar System

Cut out the words. Glue each word or phrase under "Earth," "Sun," or "Moon."

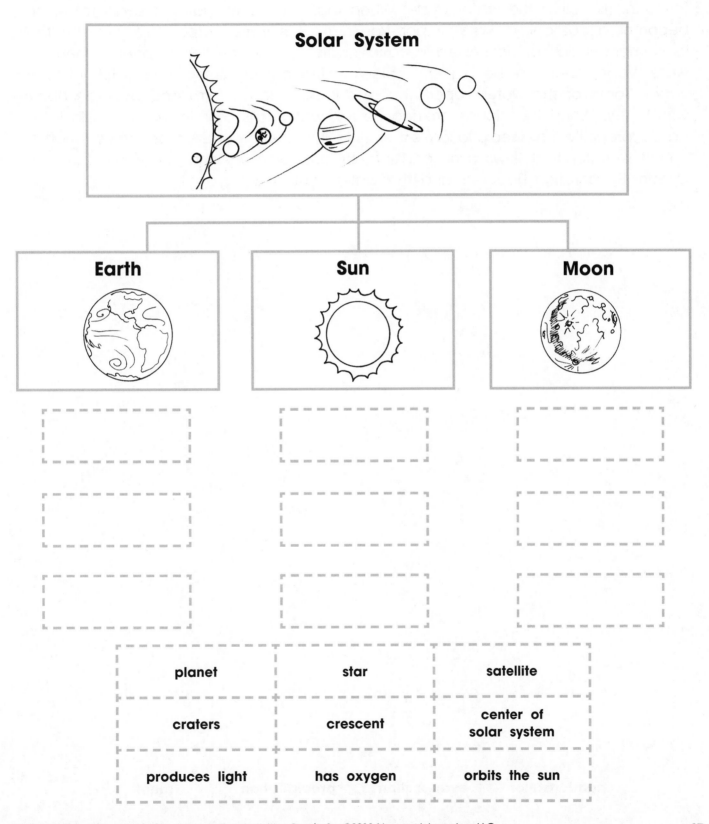

planet	star	satellite
craters	crescent	center of solar system
produces light	has oxygen	orbits the sun

Earth's Water Cycle

Read the passage. Cut out the words. Glue them in order, starting at the top.

Earth has huge amounts of water. The water is always moving and changing form. This is called the water cycle. When the sun warms water, it evaporates, or becomes a gas called water vapor. You can't see water vapor, but you can feel its dampness on hot days. Next is condensation. Condensation happens when water vapor rises into the higher, cooler air. The cooler air can't hold lots of water vapor. Some of the water vapor becomes liquid. Clouds form and become heavy with water. When the clouds are too heavy, water falls as rain or snow. This is called precipitation. Precipitation either sinks into the ground or becomes runoff. Runoff is water that flows over land into streams or rivers and finally into the ocean. Evaporation happens and the water cycle begins again.

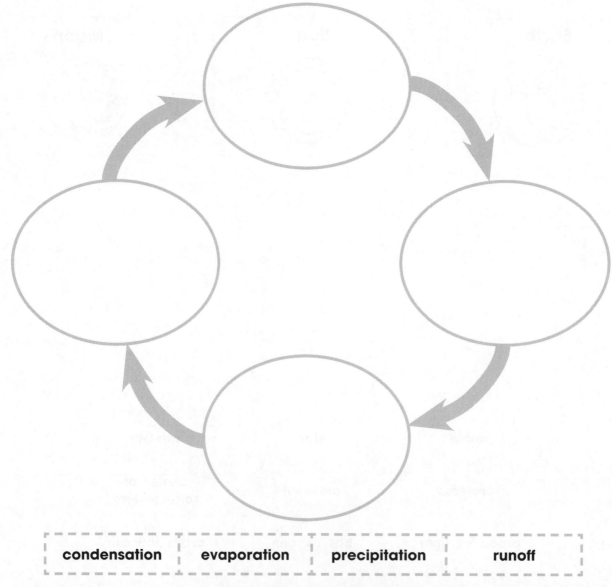

condensation   evaporation   precipitation   runoff

Earthquake!

Read the passage. Use the words in the word box to complete each sentence. Write the word or words on the line.

Earth has many layers. The outer layer is the crust. The crust includes the ground and the ocean floor. The crust is broken up into pieces called plates. Plates move all the time. The crust has many cracks, or faults, in it. When rocks get stuck along a fault, the plates keep moving. The plates push hard against the rocks. If the rock breaks, the plates move suddenly, and Earth's crust starts to shake. This is an earthquake!

Earthquakes also happen when one plate sinks under another one or when plates crash into or grind past each other.

crash	**crust**	**earthquake**	**fault**
layers	**ocean floor**	**plates**	

Earth has many _____.

The _____ is the outer layer of Earth.

Earth's crust includes the ground and the _____.

Broken pieces of Earth, or _____, move all the time.

Rocks can get stuck along a _____, or crack in the crust.

A(n) _____ happens when plates move suddenly.

Earthquakes can happen when plates _____ into each other.

Assessment

Answer the questions below by drawing a circle around the correct word.

Which is the Blue Planet?	**Earth**	**Mars**
What is the sun?	**a plane**	**a star**
How does a glacier move?	**quickly**	**slowly**
Which has craters?	**sun**	**moon**
What happens BEFORE condensation?	**precipitation**	**evaporation**
What happens AFTER precipitation?	**runoff**	**condensation**
What is broken up into plates?	**crust**	**volcanoes**
What is a fault?	**plate**	**crack**

Overview   Physical Science

Directions and Sample Answers for Activity Pages

Day 1	See "Provide a Real-World Example" below.
Day 2	Read aloud the title and directions. Help students identify the word that correctly completes each sentence. Then guide them to draw a circle around it and write it on the line. (states, properties, mass, freezes, liquid, Volume, element, atoms, molecules, temperature)
Day 3	Read aloud the title and directions. Help students label each item as a liquid, solid, or gas.
Day 4	Read aloud the title and directions. Help students read the clues and find answers in the word box. Model how to write a word into the crossword puzzle.
Day 5	Read the directions aloud. Allow time for students to complete the task. Afterward, meet individually with students to discuss their results. Use their responses to plan further instruction and review.

Provide a Real-World Example

◆ Invite students to take a look around them. **Say:** *Everything around you is matter.* Hold up a book. **Say:** *A book is matter.* Point to a desk and **say:** *A desk is matter.* Point to a couple of students and **say:** *You are matter.* Take in a deep, exaggerated breath of air and **say:** *Air is matter, too.* Turn on the faucet if there is one in your room and **say:** *Water is matter.* Write **matter** on chart paper.

◆ **Say:** *We can describe matter in thousands of ways: cold or hot, soft or hard, red, blue, green, or even invisible. But all matter is one of three states, or forms: liquid, solid, or gas. Is orange juice a solid, liquid, or gas?* (Allow responses.) *Orange juice is liquid. It has no shape. What is a computer: solid, liquid, or gas?* (Allow responses.) *A computer is a solid. It has a shape. Is the steam that comes out of a teakettle a liquid, solid, or gas?* (Allow responses.) *The steam is a gas. Like liquids, gas has no shape. This week we will explore words that have to do with all three forms of matter.* Write **solid**, **liquid**, and **gas** on the chart paper.

◆ Hand out the Day 1 activity page. Read aloud the title and directions. **Say:** *A baseball has a shape. I can feel its shape. A baseball is a solid. Let's draw a circle around the ball.* Draw attention to the next row. **Say:** *The steam that comes from my soup has no shape. But I know it is not a liquid. It must be a gas. Let's draw a circle around this choice.* Continue to guide students as needed.

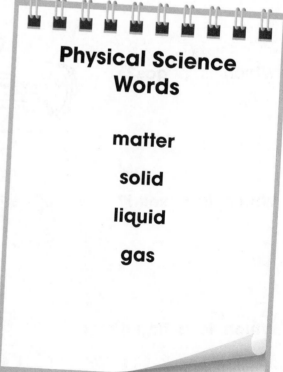

Physical Science Words

matter

solid

liquid

gas

Matter I.D.

Read the question. Draw a circle around the answer.

Which is a solid?

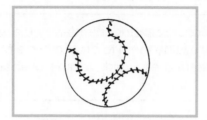 

Which is a gas?

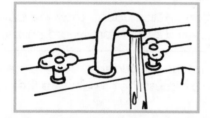 

Which is a liquid?

 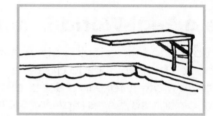

Which is a gas?

Which is a solid?

Which is a liquid?

Cloze It Up!

Read each sentence. Draw a circle around the word that correctly completes the sentence. Write it on the line.

Matter has three forms, or _____: liquid, solid, and gas.

states   gases

Size, shape, texture, and color are examples of _____ .

atoms   properties

Matter is anything that takes up space and has _____ .

liquid   mass

When water _____, it becomes a solid.

freezes   melts

When water melts, it becomes a _____ .

liquid   solid

_____ is the amount of space an object takes up.

Mass   Volume

Gold in a ring is an _____ . So is oxygen in the air.

element   atom

A pencil point has billions of _____ .

elements   atoms

Atoms join together to form _____ .

molecules   elements

A rise in _____ can change a solid into a liquid or a gas.

volume   temperature

What's the Matter?

Label the items with the correct state of matter: liquid, solid, or gas.

Name _____

Crossword

Look at the clues. Find the words in the word box. Write the answers in the crossword puzzle.

Clues

Down

1. tea is an example of this state of matter

2. the amount of space an object takes up

3. basic kinds of matter found in nature

4. anything that takes up space and has mass

Across

5. describes how an object looks, feels, and behaves

6. tiny building block of matter

7. matter that has a shape of its own

8. steam is an example of this state of matter

Word Box:
elements
gas
liquid
matter
molecule
property
solid
volume

Assessment

Draw and label an example of a solid, a liquid, and a gas in each of the boxes below.

_____

_____

_____

Overview   Multiplication

Directions and Sample Answers for Activity Pages

Day 1	See "Provide a Real-World Example" below.
Day 2	Read aloud the title and directions. Help students identify the number that correctly completes each sentence and write it on the line.
Day 3	Read aloud the title and directions. Help students identify the missing word or words in each sentence and write the word or words on the line.
Day 4	Read aloud the title and directions. Guide students to identify and draw a circle around the factors and a square around the products. Then help them identify the missing words and write them on the line.
Day 5	Read the directions aloud. Allow time for students to complete the task. Afterward, meet individually with students to discuss their results. Use their responses to plan further instruction and review.

Provide a Real-World Example

◆ Invite three volunteers to the front of the class. **Say:** *If I want to quickly know how many fingers the three of you have in total, or altogether, how could I figure it out without counting all of your fingers?* (Allow responses.) *First we need to figure out how many fingers each person has in total. Each person has five fingers on a hand and two hands, so I will multiply five fingers by two hands. Five and two are the factors, or numbers we are multiplying.* Write 5 x 2 on the board. Point to each part of the equation as you **say:** *Five multiplied by two is equal to ten. Ten is the product or answer to this first part. If each person has ten fingers, how can we figure out the total?* (Allow responses.) As you write the number sentence 10 x 3 = 30 on the board, point to each part and **say:** *Ten fingers multiplied by three people equals thirty.* **Ask:** *Which numbers are the factors?* (Allow responses.) *Ten and three are the factors.* Then ask what number is the product, and confirm that it is thirty. Write the words **total**, **multiply**, **factor**, **product**, **multiply by**, and **equals** on chart paper.

◆ Hand out the Day 1 activity page. Read aloud the title and directions. Draw attention to the first item on the left side. **Say:** *The symbol that is circled is an equal sign. It means that the left side of the equation is equal to the right side. Draw a line to the words **is equal to**.* Focus attention on the next item. **Say:** *The number circled is the product, or answer to the multiplication problem.* Continue to guide students as needed.

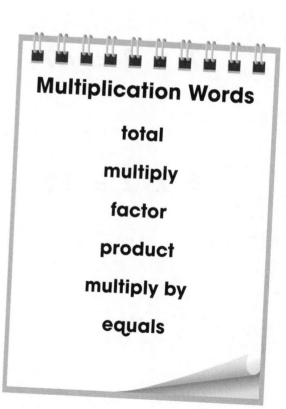

Multiplication Words

total

multiply

factor

product

multiply by

equals

Name _____

Mathematical Match-Up

Draw a line to match the items in the left column with the words and phrases in the right column.

9 x 3 = 27   equal groups

5 x 8 = 40   factors

7 x 7 = 49   is equal to

6 x 2 = 12   multiplied by

··· ··· ···   product

Equal Groups

Complete each sentence by writing the correct numerals.

3 x 2 = 6

three multiplied by two is equal to six

We see _____ equal groups.

We see _____ fish in each group.

The product or total number of fish is _____.

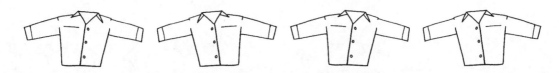

4 x 3 = 12

four multiplied by three is equal to twelve

We see _____ equal groups.

We see _____ buttons in each group.

The product or total number of buttons is _____.

2 x 5 = 10

two multiplied by five is equal to ten

We see _____ equal groups.

We see _____ bananas in each group.

The product or total number of bananas is _____.

Muffin Multiplication

Complete each sentence using the words in the word boxes.

6 x 3 = 18   Six multiplied by three is equal to eighteen.

The _____ six is a factor.

factor	number	product

The number three is also a _____.

The number eighteen is the _____.

8 x 4 = 32   Eight multiplied by four is equal to thirty-two.

The number _____ is a factor.

eight	factor	thirty-two

The number four is also a _____.

The number _____ is the product.

2 x 5 = 10   Two multiplied by five is equal to ten.

Two multiplied by five _____ ten.

five	is equal to	product

The number ten is the _____.

The number _____ is a factor.

Multiplication Mania

In the equations, draw a circle around the factors and a square around the products. Complete the sentence beneath each equation using the words in word box.

eighty	four	is equal to	multiplied by

3 x 4 = 12

Three multiplied by _____ is equal to twelve.

2 x 6 = 18

Two multiplied by six _____ eighteen.

7 x 5 = 35

Seven _____ five is equal to thirty-five.

8 x 10 = 80

Eight multiplied by ten is equal to _____.

Assessment

Draw a circle around the answers.

Which shows equal groups?

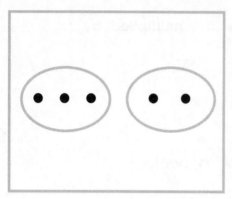 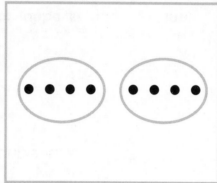 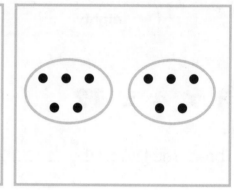

In the equation 6 x 2 = 12, which is a factor?

12   **6**   **=**

In the equation 9 x 3 = 27, which is the product?

27   **3**   **9**

Which operation would you use to solve 4 x 5?

addition   **multiplication**   **subtraction**

Which sign means equal to?

=   **x**   **>**

Which signs means to multiply?

+   **=**   **x**

Overview   Division

Directions and Sample Answers for Activity Pages

Day 1	See "Provide a Real-World Example" below.
Day 2	Read aloud the title and directions. Help students identify the number that correctly completes each sentence and write it on the line.
Day 3	Read aloud the title and directions. Help students identify the missing word or words in each sentence and write the word or words on the line.
Day 4	Read aloud the title and directions. Help students read the clues and find answers in the word box. Model how to write a word into the crossword puzzle.
Day 5	Read the directions aloud. Allow time for students to complete the task. Afterward, meet individually with students to discuss their results. Use their responses to plan further instruction and review.

Provide a Real-World Example

◆ Collect twelve pencils and put them on display. Invite six volunteers to the front of the class. **Say:** *I have 12 pencils. How can I figure out how to divide the pencils equally among the six of you?* (Allow responses.) *Since there are more pencils than people, we will divide the total number of pencils (12) by the number of kids (6).* Write *12 ÷ 6* on the board. Point to each part of the equation as you say: *Twelve is the dividend, or number to be divided. Six is the divisor, or number we are dividing by.* Using the pencils and volunteers, show how dividing twelve into six equal groups results in two pencils per group. **Say:** *The result, or quotient, of twelve divided by six is equal to two.* Write the words **divide**, **dividend**, **divisor**, **equal groups**, **quotient**, **divided by**, and **is equal to** on chart paper.

◆ Hand out the Day 1 activity page. Read aloud the title and directions. Draw attention to the first item on the left side. **Say:** *When you see this symbol in an equation, it means the number to the left of the sign is to be divided by the number to the right.* Draw a line to the words **divided by**. Focus attention on the next item. **Say:** *The number circled is the quotient, or result of dividing a number.* Continue to guide students as needed.

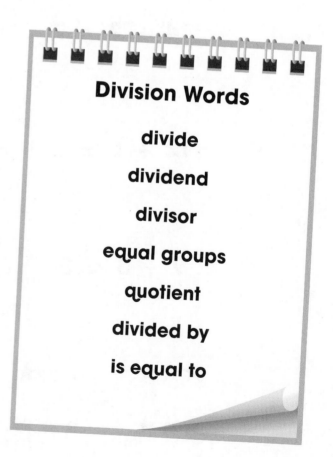

Division Words

divide

dividend

divisor

equal groups

quotient

divided by

is equal to

Name _____

Mathematical Match-Up

Draw a line to match the items in the left column with the words and phrases in the right column.

8 ÷ 2 = 4   equal groups

15 ÷ 3 = 5   dividend

14 ÷ 2 = 7   is equal to

12 ÷ 6 = 2   divided by

9 ÷ 3 = 3   quotient

   divisor

Equal Groups

Complete each sentence by writing the correct number on the line.

I see _____ hearts in all.

I see _____ rows of hearts.

I see _____ hearts in each row.

I see _____ columns of hearts.

I see _____ hearts in each column.

Twelve divided by three is equal to _____.

Twelve divided by four is equal to _____.

I see _____ pennies in all.

I see _____ rows of pennies.

I see _____ pennies in each row.

I see _____ columns of pennies.

I see _____ pennies in each column.

Ten divided by two is equal to _____.

Ten divided by five is equal to _____.

Name _____

Donut Division

Complete each sentence using the words in the word boxes.

18 ÷ 3 = 6

Eighteen divided by three is equal to six.

| dividend | divisor | quotient |

The number three is the _____.

The number six is the _____.

The number eighteen is the _____.

14 ÷ 7 = 2

Fourteen divided by seven is equal to two.

| fourteen | seven | two |

The number _____ is the divisor.

The number _____ is the quotient.

The number _____ is the dividend.

20 ÷ 5 = 4

| divided | dividend | five | four |

Twenty _____ by five is equal to four.

The number twenty is the _____.

The number _____ is the quotient.

The number _____ is the divisor.

 Unit 18 • *Everyday Vocabulary Intervention Activities Grade 3* • ©2011 Newmark Learning, LLC

Name _____

Crossword

Look at the clues. Find the words in the word box. Write the answers in the crossword puzzle.

divide
dividend
divisor
equal
four
two
quotient

Clues

Down

1. $8 \div 2 = 4$

2. what six divided by three is equal to

3. sign that shows two amounts are the same

Across

4. to separate into equal groups

5. $8 \div 2 = 4$

6. $8 \div 2 = 4$

7. what twelve divided by three is equal to

Assessment

Draw a circle around the answer.

Which pair of boxes shows equal groups?

 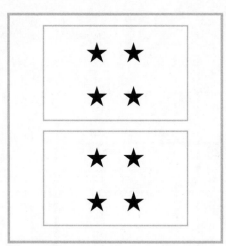 

In the equation 10 ÷ 2 = 5, which is the divisor?

10   **2**   **5**

In the equation 12 ÷ 4 = 3, which is the quotient?

3   **12**   **4**

In the equation 15 ÷ 3 = 5, which is the dividend?

5   **3**   **15**

Which operation would you use to solve 4 ÷ 2?

addition   **multiplication**   **division**

Which sign means equal to?

=   **x**   **÷**

Overview Fractions

Directions and Sample Answers for Activity Pages

Day 1	See "Provide a Real-World Example" below.
Day 2	Read aloud the title and directions. Help students cut out the pictures and identify each as one-half, one-third, or one-fourth, and glue it in the correct column.
Day 3	Read aloud the title and directions. Help students identify the missing word or words in each sentence and write the word or words on the line.
Day 4	Read aloud the title and directions. Help students make a match between the items in the left column and the words in the right column.
Day 5	Read the directions aloud. Allow time for students to complete the task. Afterward, meet individually with students to discuss their results. Use their responses to plan further instruction and review.

Provide a Real-World Example

◆ **Ask:** *How many students are in our class?* (Allow responses.) Write the number on the board. Draw a bar above it. Then **say:** *Raise your hand if you have brown hair.* Count aloud the number of students raising their hands. Write that number above the bar to create a fraction. Point to the bottom number and **say:** *Our class has a total of (number) students.* Now point to the top number and **say:** *(Number) students in our whole class have brown hair.* Point to the fraction and **say:** *This is a fraction. A fraction describes parts of a whole. This fraction tells what part of our whole class of students has brown hair.* Point to the bottom number again and **say:** *The number below the bar is the denominator. It tells the total number of equal parts into which the whole has been divided. In this case, each student is an equal part.* Point to the top number and **say:** *The number above the bar is the numerator. It tells how many of the equal parts of the whole are being considered. In this case, the numerator is the number of students with brown hair. They are part of the whole.* Write **equal parts**, **fraction**, **whole**, **numerator**, and **denominator** on chart paper.

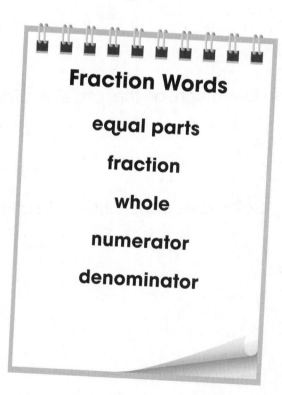

Fraction Words

equal parts

fraction

whole

numerator

denominator

◆ Hand out the Day 1 activity page. Read aloud the title and directions. Count aloud the parts of the circle. **Say:** *The circle is divided into three equal parts. Let's write the numeral 3 below the bar on the fraction. Remember, the total number of equal parts is called the denominator.* Now count aloud the shaded parts. **Say:** *One part is shaded. Let's write the numeral 1 above the bar on the fraction. The 1 is called the numerator. It tells how much of the whole is shaded.* Read aloud the question. Allow students to answer. Then **say:** *We call this fraction one-third because there are three equal parts in total, and one is shaded.* Guide students through the second part of the activity page as needed.

Name _____

Parts of a Whole

Write the fraction. Then answer the question.

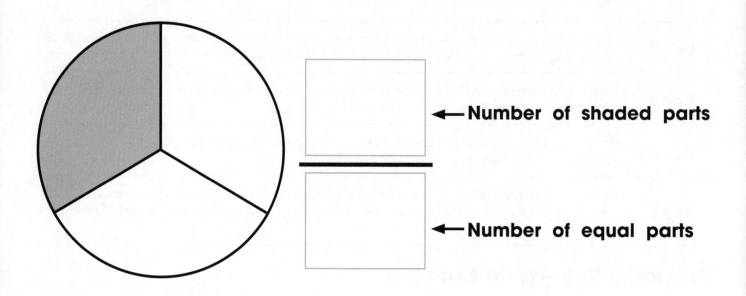

←**Number of shaded parts**

←**Number of equal parts**

How much of the circle is shaded?   **one-fourth   one-half   one-third**

Color one part. Write a fraction. _____

How much of the whole is shaded?   **one-fourth   one-half   one-third**

Fraction I.D.

Cut out the pictures. Glue each under the fraction that it shows.

1/2 one-half	1/3 one-third	1/4 one-fourth

Get Set

Complete each sentence using the words in the word boxes.

    $\dfrac{3}{4}$

denominator	four
three	set

The set has a total of _____ hearts.

The _____ has a total of three shaded hearts.

The _____ is four.

The numerator is _____ .

     $\dfrac{2}{5}$

five	numerator
set	two

The _____ has a total of five cars.

The set has a total of _____ shaded cars.

The denominator is _____ .

The _____ is two.

 $\dfrac{1}{4}$

equal parts	four
one	one-fourth

The pizza has four _____ .

_____ of the pizza has mushrooms.

The numerator is _____ .

The denominator is _____ .

Name _____

Fraction Match-Up

Draw a line to match the items in the left column with the words and phrases in the right column.

$\dfrac{1}{2}$ one-third

$\dfrac{④}{5}$ denominator

$2\dfrac{1}{2}$ equal parts

                    numerator

$\dfrac{1}{4}$ one-half

$\dfrac{2}{⑤}$ mixed number

$\dfrac{1}{3}$ one-fourth

40   whole number

Assessment

Draw a circle around the answers.

Which shows the fraction one-half?

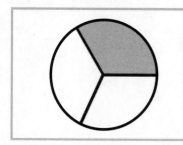 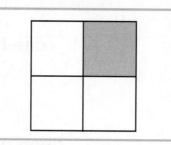 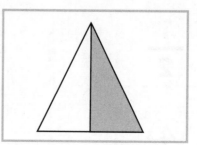

Which fraction is one-third?

$\frac{1}{3}$ $\qquad$ $\frac{1}{2}$ $\qquad$ $\frac{1}{4}$

In the fraction $\frac{2}{5}$, which number is the denominator?

2 $\qquad$ **7** $\qquad$ **5**

In the fraction $\frac{3}{4}$, which number is the numerator?

3 $\qquad$ **4** $\qquad$ **7**

Which set shows one-fourth?

Color in one-third of the set.

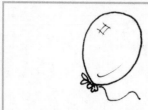  

Overview Geometry

Directions and Sample Answers for Activity Pages

Day 1	See "Provide a Real-World Example" below.
Day 2	Read aloud the title and directions. Help students read the clues and find answers in the word box. Model how to write a word into the crossword puzzle.
Day 3	Read aloud the title and directions. Help students count the sides of each polygon and number them in the order of fewest sides to most sides. (triangle, rhombus, pentagon, hexagon, heptagon, octagon)
Day 4	Read aloud the title and directions. Help students identify the missing word in each sentence and write it on the line.
Day 5	Read the directions aloud. Allow time for students to complete the task. Afterward, meet individually with students to discuss their results. Use their responses to plan further instruction and review.

Provide a Real-World Example

◆ Bring a symmetrical leaf in preparation for this unit as well as pictures of other natural objects that have symmetry, such as a butterfly and a snowflake. Project the leaf for students to see up close. Using your finger, draw an imaginary line down the center of the leaf and **ask:** *What do you notice about the two sides of the leaf?* (Allow responses.) *One half of the leaf looks like the mirror image of the other half. That is because the leaf has symmetry. The imaginary line I drew down the center is called a line of symmetry.* Write the words **symmetry** and **line of symmetry** on chart paper.

◆ Pass around the pictures you brought in. **Say:** *Symmetry is everywhere in nature—in flowers, snowflakes, even in butterflies. What have you seen in nature that has symmetry?*

◆ Draw a rectangle on the board. Remind students that a polygon is a closed figure with three or more straight sides. Write **polygon** on the chart paper. **Say:** *Polygons have symmetry, too. A rectangle has two lines of symmetry.* Draw a line down the center of the rectangle. Now draw a line across the center of the rectangle, from left to right. Draw a square on the board. **Ask:** *How many lines of symmetry does a square have?* (Allow responses.) Then demonstrate how a square has four lines of symmetry. Write **rectangle** and **square** on the chart paper.

◆ Hand out the Day 1 activity page. Read aloud the title and directions. **Say:** *The two sides of the trapezoid are exactly the same. The trapezoid has symmetry. Circle the trapezoid.* Continue to guide students through the activity as needed.

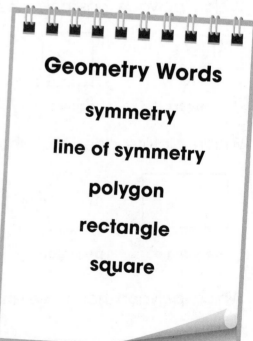

Geometry Words

symmetry

line of symmetry

polygon

rectangle

square

Which Has Symmetry?

Read each question. Draw a circle around the answer.

Which polygon shows the correct line of symmetry?

trapezoid   **heart**   **parallelogram**

Which shape has two lines of symmetry?

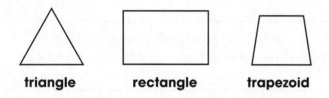

triangle   **rectangle**   **trapezoid**

How many lines of symmetry does a square have?
two   three   four

square

Which polygon has only one line of symmetry?

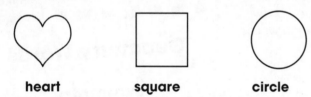

heart   **square**   **circle**

Which picture does NOT show a line of symmetry?

rectangle   **pentagon**   **arrow**

Which polygon has three lines of symmetry?

**equilateral
triangle**   **rhombus**   **rectangle**

Name _____

Polygon Crossword

Look at the clues. Find the words in the word box. Write the answers in the crossword puzzle.

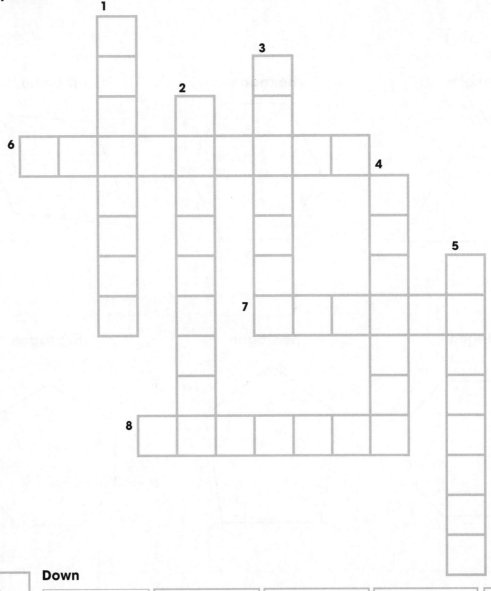

Word box:
- hexagon
- octagon
- pentagon
- rectangle
- rhombus
- square
- trapezoid
- triangle

Down

1.
2.
3.
4.
5.

Across

6.
7.
8.

Side by Side

Look at the polygons. Number them in order from fewest sides to most sides.

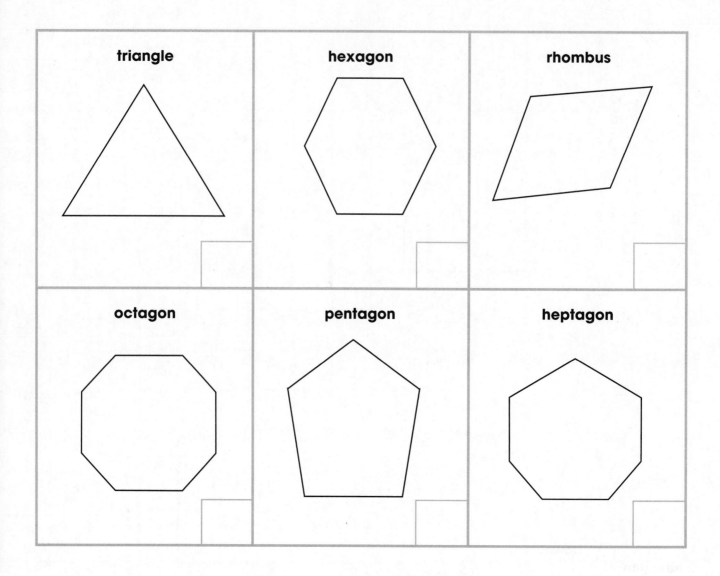

| triangle | hexagon | rhombus |
| octagon | pentagon | heptagon |

Shape Up!

Complete each sentence using the words in the word box. Write the words on the line.

angles	congruent	five	four	octagon
pentagon	polygon	size	three	trapezoid

A(n) _____ has five sides.

A pentagon has _____ angles.

A trapezoid has _____ sides.

A(n) _____ has four angles.

An octagon is a(n) _____

A(n) _____ has eight sides.

An octagon has eight _____.

The triangles are the same shape and _____.

The triangles are _____.

The triangles have _____ sides and three angles.

Assessment

Complete each sentence using the words in the word box. Write each word on the line.

| size | shape | polygons | equal | four | hexagon | line of symmetry |

Congruent polygons are the same _____ and _____.

A _____ has six sides.

A pentagon has one _____.

A square and a rhombus both have _____ angles.

A triangle, trapezoid, and octagon are all _____.

A rectangle and a rhombus have a(n) _____ number of sides.

Draw lines of symmetry for each shape.

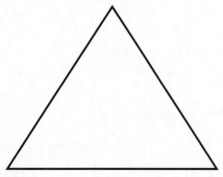  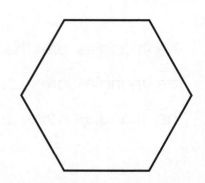

Unit 20 • Everyday Vocabulary Intervention Activities Grade 3 • ©2011 Newmark Learning, LLC